The Hispanic Hybrid Identity in Miami: Ethnographic Description and Missiological Implications

Enoch Wan and J. David Lopez

Diaspora Series of CDRR

The Hispanic Hybrid Identity in Miami:
Ethnographic Description and Missiological Implications

Enoch Wan and J. David Lopez

Cover designed by Mark Benec

Published by the Center of Diaspora and Relational Research (CDRR)
Western Academic Publishers
5511 SE Hawthorne Blvd., Portland, OR 97215, USA

ISBN- 978-1-954692-04-6

***

Western Academic
Publishers

TABLE OF CONTENTS

LIST OF FIGURES

CHAPTER 1

INTRODUCTION

The Purpose of the Book

The purpose of this book is twofold: providing an ethnographic description of the Hispanic hybrid (HH) identity found in Miami-Dade County and deriving missiological implications from the ethnographic data.

The Background of the Book

The research for this book was done by David Lopez for his dissertation at Western Seminary entitled "An Ethnographic Study of the Hispanic Hybrid Identity in Miami"[1] under the supervision of Enoch Wan in 2019. Then the two co-authored this book in order to share the research findings with the Christian community. This book is part of both "Series of Relational Research" and "Series of Diaspora Studies" (Center for Diaspora and Relational Research), Western Seminary Press.

Definition of Key Terms

1st Generation Hispanic (G1) – First wave of immigrants arriving into the U.S.A. who have left their homeland, for whichever reason, and ended up living in Miami as their place of residence.

1.5 Generation Hispanic (G1.5) – Referring to children who immigrated to Miami prior to the age of 12 and grew up in Miami. These have high identification with homeland cultural and ethnic values as well as U.S.A. cultural and ethnic values and are fully bilingual and bicultural.

2nd Generation Hispanic (G2) – Referring to children of immigrants (G1 or G1.5) who were born in Miami. These have shared cultural and ethnic values and cultures of other Hispanic ethnicities found within proximity; may be bilingual and bicultural.

Emic – A description of behavior or a belief in terms meaningful (consciously or unconsciously) to the researcher; that is, the account is coming from a person within the culture.

---

[1] ...ez.

Ethnography – A description of a culture; in this case, the Hispanic diaspora culture.

Hispanics – Persons whose origins can be traced to Latin America and the Caribbean.

Hispanic diaspora – All the generations and expressions of Hispanics and their children who have immigrated to Miami Florida because of internal or external pressures in their home countries.

Hispanic Hybridity (HH) – A reference to the fusing of Hispanic identities found in Miami-Dade County promoting the development of interethnic blending which results in new cultural identity.

Hispanic Hybrid Identity – The emergence of cultural and social norms attributed to the children of Hispanic immigrants born in Miami that have developed through a combination of shared life circumstance, experiences, cultural proximity, cultural blending, and interethnic relationships.

Hybridity – The fusion of two or more distinct entities. Ethnic hybridity is the result of cross-cultural ethnic contact which often occurs across national borders as well as across cultural and generational boundaries, which leads to the development of a new, multidimensional identity that may complement or seemingly contradict another.

Intercultural Theory – an explanation of how people from different ethnic and cultural backgrounds adapt to each other in day-to-day encounters.

Interculturation – the composite fusing which takes place between two or more cultures.

Mixed-methods – research which specifically includes the mixing of qualitative and quantitative approaches.

Spanglish – The outcome of blending English and Spanish languages resulting in a new dialect that is spoken among and understood primarily by the G1.5s and G2s.

Transnational – the global migration experience of common people, families, and their extended families from one culture or country to another.

Trans-Ethnic – refers to identifying as a member of an ethnic, cultural, or national group other than the category one belongs to in terms of social, state, and/or other forces.

Trans-Ethnic Leadership – refers to the one who is able to navigate through the convergence of various ethnic blends in terms of social, state, and/or other forces.

The Organization of the Book

This book begins with an Introduction (Chapter 1) followed by information of theoretical and historical background in Chapter 2. Chapter 3 is a simple explanation of the research methodology and data collection process. The major content of this book – Chapter 4 – is an ethnographic description of the Hispanic hybrid identity found in Miami-Dade County. Chapter 5 covers Hispanic hybrids: relational and cultural identities. The book will conclude with Chapter 7, after missiological implications derived from the research findings of Chapter 6.

CHAPTER 2

THEORETICAL AND HISTORICAL BACKGROUND

Introduction

The foundation for this ethnographic study was drawn from differing sources of literature from varying fields of study.[2]

Thematic literature forms the first section of the literature review. Specific emphasis was made on how culture in Miami has been shaped by domestic and international influence. The literature review drew from books, articles, and journals which discuss the diaspora history of Hispanics in Miami. Theoretical literature forms the second section. This section covers the matter of ethnic identity and will introduce Hispanic Hybridity. The final section of the literature review discusses the area of methodology. In this section, literature on varying methods is used to highlight a mixed methods approach.

In Miami immigration is a constant. Learning how to understand and engage the various expressions of immigration is the challenge. Some of those expressions can be categorized as shown in the table below:

Status	
Illegal/undocumented	Student
Refugee	Investor/Entrepreneur
Exile	Citizen
Resident	**Traveler**

Figure 1. Expressions of Immigration

Along with new immigration, the G1.5 and G2 generation Hispanics are immigrant children. These grow up in the U.S.A. and become more distant from their home culture, yet not completely integrated into what is recognized as typical North American culture.

[2] Lopez, chapter 2.

G1	1st Generation Hispanic
G1.5	1.5 Generation Hispanic
G2	2nd Generation Hispanic
HH	Hispanic Hybrid(s)

Figure 2. Abbreviations used in this book

A result is the blending of cultures that led towards the emergence of an identity of Hispanic Hybridity.[3] It was the desire of the researcher to develop an ethnographic understanding of the "in between" generations that have been and are currently emerging. The above two diagrams illustrate various points of contact which lead to the emergence and "blooming" of Hispanic hybrids in Miami-Dade with the three largest populations of Hispanic immigrants as base for this ethnographic study.

Hispanic Themes: A Brief Study of Acculturation, Interculturation, and Hybridity Theories

Researchers of cultural psychology have defined ethnic identity as a dynamic multidimensional construct that may evolve over time.[4] The development of one's ethnic identity may involve one's subjective feelings toward a culture, heritage, cultural labels an individual pragmatically applies to his or her identity, a sense of belongingness to the culture, the salience of the cultural perspective, and the majority of the population's opinion regarding the ethnic group.[5] The HH in Miami is an expression of this identity. When the different cultural and ethnic groups found in Miami come into contact with each other, after sufficient time, they engage in mutual exchange of cultural traits to produce a new hybrid culture. This construct is the result of intercultural grafting which has occurred between various Hispanic cultures with each other and with the host culture of the U.S.A.

The term "enculturation" is "the process by which individuals learn the norms, values, and expected behaviors of the society into which they were born." "Acculturation," on the other hand, means "acquiring the values and

---

[3] Marwan M. Kraidy, *Hybridity or the Cultural Logic of Globalization* (Philadelphia, PA: Temple University Press, 2005), 5.

[4] J.S. Phinney, "Ethnic Identity and Acculturation, in *Acculturation: Advances in Theory, Measurement, and Applied Research,* ed. K. Chun, P. Organista, and G. Marin (Washington, DC: American Psychological Association, 2003), 63-81.

[5] C. L. Costigan, C. M. Koryzma, J. M. Hua, and L. J. Chance, "Ethnic Identity, Achievement, and Psychological Adjustment: Examining Risk and Resilience among Youth from Immigrant Chinese Families in Canada," *Cultural Diversity and Ethnic Minority Psychology* 16, no. 2 (April 2010): 264–73. https://doi.org/10.1037/a0017275.

norms with conformed behaviors of host culture after emigration."[6] Acculturation is what is generally expected of people who have immigrated to the U.S.A., intend to remain, and seek citizenship. Their children will be enculturated by learning the language, norms, and values of their parents' original culture and, at the same time, acculturated by the American educational system, the media, and social interactions with other children.

The fusing of Hispanic identities is a part of the Hispanic dimension of G1, G2s, and the emerging HH. The development of the HH was observed through the lens of developing an ethnic identity. As the varying Hispanic identities in Miami were considered, various theories were taken into consideration.

All persons everywhere are affected by their environment. In the Ecological Systems Theory,[7] one sees an approach that demonstrates how the development of children is affected by their social relationship and the world around them. This theory holds to the idea that a person's development, specifically that of children, is deeply affected and influenced by everything in their surrounding environment. In particular, environment is divided into five different levels, as shown in the diagram below.

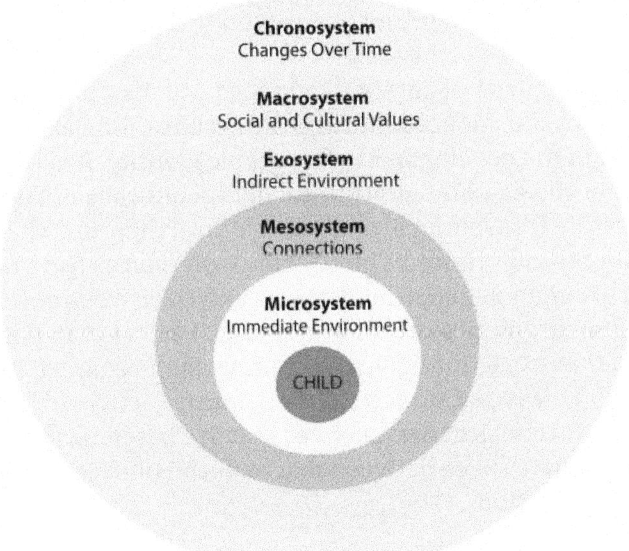

Figure 3. Brofenbrenner's Ecological Systems Theory

---

[6] Maria D.Thomson and Laurie Hoffman-Goetz, "Defining and measuring acculturation: A systematic review of public health studies with Hispanic populations in the United States," *Social Science & Medicine* 69, no. 7 (October 2009): 983-91. https://doi.org/10.1016/j.socscimed.2009.05.011.

[7] Urie Bronfenbrenner, "Ecological Systems Theory," in *Annals of Child Development*, vol. 6, ed. Ross Vasta, *International Encyclopedia of Education*, ed. Torsten Husen and T. Neville Postlewaite (London: Jessica Kingsley Publisher, 1989), 187–249.

Drawing from Brofenbrenner's work matters because the HH is present in adolescence and young adulthood. In this theory, children find themselves simultaneously enmeshed in different ecosystems. Each of these systems inevitably interacts with and influences each other and every aspect of the child's life. There is no clear break between the ecosystems, thus each one blends with the other. In Hispanic youth, there are two critical components that contribute toward the development of their ethnic identities: (1) Parental involvement, and (2) Discrimination experiences. These two factors impact the blending of ecology points in Brofenbrenner's work.

Parental involvement has a significant impact on the formation of one's ethnic identity. Scholars suggest that an important role of family is to help children learn values and behaviors that allow them to adapt to the environment in which they live.[8] Furthermore, among ethnic families, parents' attempts to teach their children about their ethnicity are considered essential for ensuring their children's optimal adaptation.[9] Among Hispanic families the influence of parents may be particularly salient given the cultural emphasis on obedience to parents and respect for authority. Although there is much diversity within Hispanic families, scholars suggest that values emphasizing family, or a strong orientation and connection to family, are one of the key values transmitted across generations.[10]

Along with the impact of parental influence and discriminatory experiences, there is evidence that suggests acculturation also plays a significant role in the development of an ethnic identity. It is necessary to go further than the universal integration and multiculturalism. Two approaches considered are the transnational and intercultural theories. The *transnational* approach analyzes migrations as globalizing experiences from the bottom, as globalization of common people, of families and their webs of relations. In this perspective, immigrants are considered as social actors that, within the resources and the restrictions given to them from the contexts they operate, elaborate their choices and projects, they define objectives and they try to achieve them.[11] Sociological perspectives that are based on this concept are set in an intermediate space between macro-social interpretations and micro or individual explanations.

---

[8] R. D. Parke and R. Buriel, "Socialization in the Family: Ecological and Ethnic Perspectives," in *Handbook of Child Psychology,* ed. W. Damon (New York, NY: Wiley Publishers, 1998), 3:463–552.

[9] S. Marshall, "Ethnic Socialization of African American Children: Implications for Parenting, Identity Development, and Academic Achievement," *Journal of Youth and Adolescence* 24, no. 4 (August 1995): 377–96.

[10] F. Sabogal, G. Marin, R. Otero-Sabogal, B. Marin, and E. J. Perez-Stable, "Hispanic Familism and Acculturation: What Changes and What Doesn't?" *Hispanic Journal of Behavioral Sciences* 9, no. 4 (December 1987): 397–412, https//doi.org/10.1177/07399863870094003.

[11] Roger D. Waldinger, "Between 'Here' and 'There': Immigrant Cross-Border Activities and Loyalties," *International Migration Review* 42, no. 1 (March 2008): 3–29 https://doi.org/10.1111/j.1747-7379.2007.00112.x.

The transnational model leads to redefining the concept of the relationship between hosting society and the maintenance of transnational bonds of immigrants. Migrations contribute in eroding traditional frontiers among languages, cultures, ethnic groups, and states-nations. They challenge cultural traditions, national identities, and political institutions.[12] In this sense, the transnational theory is linked to the perspective of intercultural integration. This kind of model goes in the direction of conceptual encounters of immigrants and natives, in a process of openness towards diversity, confrontation, and exchange. Interculturalism is set further than assimilationism and differentialism and considers the dialogue of different cultures and identities. An intercultural approach takes into consideration interaction, mixing, and hybridity between cultural communities.[13]

Intercultural theory is based on the dynamic conception of culture and on a multidimensional reading of the ethnic-cultural identity. The word is derived from the Latin "inter" (between) and "cultural" (culture). "Interculturation" is the sum of all relations and interactions between different cultures, through meetings, and debates. This presumes intercultural exchange is founded on dialogue, mutual respect, and the desire to preserve the cultural identity of each one. Interculturation is a temporal and spatial process.[14]

The intercultural perspective substitutes a static, historic, and social vision of cultures. This is a progressive, dynamic, situated, and social conception that grasps the dialogue between different cultures. Hispanic hybridity is an emerging expression of interculturation. The fusing occurred and is continuing to occur around ethnic lines that are blending culture, language, and socio-economics. The result is not simply a composite expression of Hispanic, but one that is also formed and informed by the host U.S.A. culture.

Members of these ethnic groups do not necessarily give up their own culture, rather participate in various ways in each other's culture. It is viewed as the locale of human spatial behavior, where the culture of origin is mixed with new cultural elements and identity to occupy a new temporal and spatial locale. It does so without exhausting openness toward the others and further engages the presence of others. It also includes the capability of the host community to influence and be influenced, beyond their current parameter of location and time. Interculturation invites newcomers to accept and to abide in the existing structures of the host community, which leads them towards a functional and social integration.

---

[12] Steven Vertovec, "Migration and other Modes of Transnationalism: Toward Conceptual Cross-Fertilization," *International Migration Review* 37, no. 3 (Fall 2003): 641-65, https://doi.org/10.1111/j.1747-7379.2003.tb00153.x.

[13] Rina Manuela Contini, "New Generations and Intercultural Integration in Multi-Ethnic Society," *Procedia – Social and Behavioral Sciences* 93 (October 2013): 1820, https://doi.org/10.1016/j.sbspro.2013.10.124.

[14] For detail discussion on time and space, see E. T. Hall, *The Dance of Life, the Other Dimension of Time.* (London: Anchor Books, 1989).

"Interculturation" is not "multiculturism" in that the latter is a description of a phenomenon of several cultures co-existing together without any mutual sharing or assimilation. It is different from acculturation which infers the modification of the culture of a group or of persons under the influence of another culture. It is the opposite of pluralism, a system whereby different ways of thinking are accepted so that people remain as individuals with no connection between them. Interculturation is, on the contrary, openness to the diversity of others. It comes down to the way one sees the other and, from him, seeing oneself. It is the culture of understanding the human person. Originally, interculturation concerned chiefly the phenomenon of migration. Actually, the term first appeared in the 1970s in Europe concerning the integration of migrants.[15] Then, it was extended to include every rupture of culture and can be applied to all types: ethnic, national, religion, generation, or social group.

The intercultural perspective substitutes a static, historic, and social vision of cultures. This is a progressive, dynamic, situated, and social conception that grasps the dialogue between different cultures. Hispanic hybridity is an emerging expression of interculturation. The fusing occurred and is continuing to occur around ethnic lines that are blending culture, language, and socio-economics. The result was not just a composite expression of Hispanic, but one that was also formed and informed by the host U.S.A. culture.

For purposes of the HH and Hispanic migratory patterns, data suggests an associating of selective acculturation with greater transnational involvement, with some limited evidence of downward assimilation associated with higher rates of sending financial assistance among some nationalities. The different ethnicities that live in Miami are not inter-dependent; rather they are more inter-ethnic cohabitants that are confined to the same space. A distinction needs to be made between selective acculturation and consonant acculturation. The former has a higher association with its culture of origin as it is immigrant by choice. The latter does not have a high level of involvement as these immigrants have chosen to leave due to negative factors such as poverty, instability in government, war, or a poor financial infrastructure.[16] This is one of the bases for the HH. This dimension of the HH can be broken into three categories: (1) Locals, (2) Exiles, and (3) Mobiles.

Locals are those who consider Miami to be their hometown, roughly 20% of the population. **Exiles** are those who find themselves in Miami because of political or economic necessity. They are generally in Miami waiting for political change to occur in their home country. **Mobiles** do not identify with

---

[15] S. J. Mason, "L'Église ouverte sur le monde," *Nouvelle Revue Théologiquê*, (1962): 84.
[16] William Haller and Patricia Landolt, "The Transnational Dimensions of Identity Formation: Adult Children of Immigrants in Miami," *Ethnic and Racial Studies* 28, no. 6 (November 2005): 1182-1214, https://doi.org/10.1080/01419870500224554.

Miami as home and like exiles, do not consider their stay in Miami permanent. Unlike exiles, mobiles have come to Miami by choice, and they can leave by choice because of affluence. Compared to other metropolitan areas, many of Miami's foreign immigrants belong to the upper income classes. Nijman refers to this mixture of identities as the "dynamic and plural nature of processes of identity formation."[17]

Themes Addressing History of Hispanics in the United States, Florida, and Miami

In the United States, before there was New England, there was New Spain. Before Boston, there was Santa Fe. The teaching of American history normally emphasizes the founding and growth of the British colonies in North America, their emergence as an independent nation in 1776, and the development of the United States from east to west. This treatment easily omits the fact that there was significant colonization by Spain of what is now the American Southwest from the 16th century onward. It also tends to ignore, until the Mexican War is mentioned, that the whole Southwest, from Texas westward to California, was a Spanish-speaking territory with its own distinctive heritage, culture, and customs for many decades.

The Spanish-speaking citizens of the United States who were incorporated into the country as a result of the Mexican War are called Mexican Americans. Their numbers have since increased as a result of immigration. Other Spanish-speaking citizens came from Cuba and Puerto Rico, and smaller numbers are immigrants from Central and South America and from the Dominican Republic. Taken together, these people are called Hispanics, or Latinos.

Summary

The theoretical and historical background of Hispanic hybrid (HH) identity has been briefly presented in this chapter. This basic understanding is important prior to detailed and in-depth study of the subject matter of the book.

---

[17] Jan Nijman, "Locals, Exiles, and Cosmopolitans: A Theoretical Argument about Identity and Places in Miami," *Journal of Economic and Social Geography* 98, no. 2 (April 2007): 176-87, https://doi.org/10.1111/j.1467-9663.2007.00390.x.

CHAPTER 3

RESEARCH METHODOLOGY AND DATA COLLECTION

Introduction

This section is intended to highlight the mixed-methods that were used toward developing an ethnographic study of the HH in Miami. According to John W. Creswell, of University of Nebraska:

Mixed methods is a research approach, popular in the social, behavioral, and health sciences, in which researchers collect, analyze, and integrate both quantitative and qualitative data in a single study or in a sustained long-term program of inquiry to address their research questions.[18]

The result of this study is a qualitative ethnographic work, preceded by initial survey (quantitative – phase 1) and pilot study (phase 2). The focus of this book is on the emerging HH in Miami, Florida. Once the subject matter had been limited by population size, the ethnographic questions ensued with the research participants. Data collection occurred by administering and capturing HH survey results, recording interviews, drawing data from books, journals, articles, participant observation, and the researcher's emic understanding of the HH. Data analysis was the next step towards the development of an ethnographic study. Once analyzed, an ethnographic record was written.

Research Methodology

A mixed-methods approach was used for the development of this ethnographic study. The literature cited for the research methodology was used to shape the quantitative (see Appendix 1 and Appendix 2) and qualitative research questions (see Appendix 3). These works provided guidance in the development of the survey, survey delivery, data collection, research organization, field questions, and interpretation of qualitative data.

---

[18] John W. Creswell, "Steps in Conducting a Scholarly Mixed Methods Study," presentation November 14, 2013, DigitalCommons@University of Nebraska – Lincoln, accessed April 1, 2020, https://digitalcommons.unl.edu/dberspeakers/48/.

Research occurred in the following sequence:

Phase One – Electronic Online Survey
Phase Two –

- Pilot Study
- Semi structured interviews of initial ethnographic questions

Phase Three –

- Ethnographic study
- Refined Semi-structured interviews

Phase Four – Data Analysis

The following table lists out the sequence and detailed description.

<table>
<tr><th>Research Phases of the Ethnographic Development</th><th>Participants (Men/Women who may be single/married/divorced)</th><th>Means of Research</th></tr>
<tr><td>Phase One – Electronic Online Survey</td><td>72 persons</td><td>Online Google Drive Survey</td></tr>
<tr><td>Phase Two – Pilot Study
Semi structured interviews with initial ethnographic questions</td><td>4 persons that fit the HH criteria were interviewed in a semi-structured format for a period of 90 minutes</td><td rowspan="2">Reflective notes were taken by researcher
Coding for Themes
Mobile/Tablet devices with audio recording capabilities
Field notes and memos</td></tr>
<tr><td>Phase Three – Ethnographic Study
Refined Semi-structured interviews</td><td>5 persons who fit the HH criteria were interviewed twice in a semi-structured format for a period of 90 minutes each time</td></tr>
<tr><td>Phase Four - Data Analysis</td><td>An ethnographic study was produced</td><td>All phase three interviews were transcribed and analyzed for any emerging themes or for confirmation of hypothesis</td></tr>
</table>

Figure 4. Research Methodology Sequence

Data Collection

The information gathered was the basis for developing the ethnographic study of the HH in Miami. The focus was to understand the emerging HH in

Miami along with providing suggestions for cross cultural leaders. Currently, all findings in this ethnographic study are drawn from mostly subjective data based on the interviews of the qualifying research participants. All findings are written from an emic perspective.

The research for this work occurred in multiple phases. First, there was an electronic survey that was sent to seventy-two people to determine if they fit the limitations as described above. The researcher created and administered the survey. This was the quantitative portion of the research. The intent of the survey was to identify the best candidates for the interview phase of the research. From that initial set, participants were narrowed down to nine persons. Based on the survey results, these nine persons were the ones that most fit the description of the HH being studied; some single, some married. Of the nine, four of them were selected as the pilot phase of the research. At this point the interview questions were initially administered, tested, and refined. The researcher followed the Spradley ethnographic research cycle that is illustrated below.

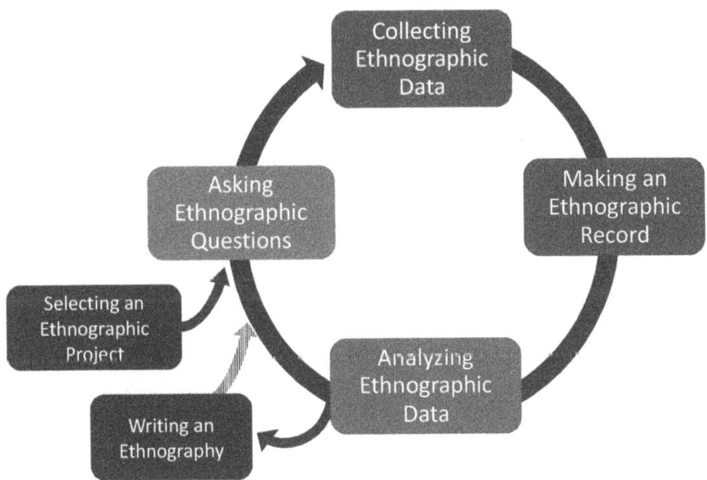

Figure 5. Ethnographic Research Cycle[19]

[19] Adapted from James P. Spradley, *Participant Observation* (New York: Holt, Rhinehart & Winston Inc., 1980).

Once the interview questions were refined, the researcher scheduled a time with the five phase two participants for an interview session. The researcher anticipated semi-structured interviewing sessions with each individual, at times as a couple, to gather sufficient data to be able to address the research questions mentioned above. Along with the research findings, the researcher also wrote from an emic perspective. The researcher used a version of the chart below for data tracking, collection, and thematic findings.

- Participant 1 – Male (RD). His parents were born in Cuba. RD was born and raised in Miami.
- Participant 2 – Female (BS). Her parents were born in Cuba. BS was born and raised in Miami.
- Participant 3 – Female (IG). Her parents were born in Nicaragua. IG was born and raised in Miami.
- Participant 4 – Female (AM). Her parents were born in Cuba. AM was born and raised in Miami.
- Participant 5 – Male (GM). His parents were born in Cuba. GM was born and raised in Miami.
- Participant 6 – Female (CB). Her parents were born in Cuba. CB was born and raised in Miami.
- Participant 7 – Female (KLP). Her parents were born in Cuba and Colombia. KLP was born and raised in Miami.
- Participant 8 – Male (SG). His parents were born in Cuba. SG was born and raised in Miami.
- Participant 9 – Female (AC). Her mother was born in Miami, she is of Cuban descent. Her father was born in Colombia. AC was born in Miami, FL.
- Participant 10 – The researcher will be informing the ethnography from an emic

Figure 6. Hispanic Hybrid Research Participants

Data Collection in a Series of Phases

Phase One: Initial Survey

The survey was administered by the researcher through an online survey that was emailed to the participant. This survey was created using Google drive; all online survey data was captured and collected on the same drive. From this drive, the findings were generated into a quantitative graph to determine which participants qualified for phase two of the research.

Phase Two: Pilot Study

Four of the participants were exposed to the initial draft of questions in the Pilot Phase of the interview. Based on these initial interviews, the researcher refined the questions as necessary in order to generate the best and most accurate content for the research. These interviews were recorded using the mediums described in Figure 7. All interviews were transcribed. While data was being collected in the pilot phase, interview questions were refined and refocused.

Phase Three: Series of Four Ethnographic Interviews

A series of redefined ethnographic questions was asked in order to allow participants to explain their experience in their own terms. Their thoughts were recorded for later content analysis. The aim of the in-depth interview was to capture the following as reported by the participants: (1) Words, (2) Descriptions, and (3) Thoughts and Feelings. To keep track of key points, reoccurring cultural themes, or new ideas that may reframe the research, the researcher used the following methods to collect and record:

Mobile devices with audio recording capabilities	Tablets with audio recording devices	Field notes and memos taken by the researcher	Reflective notes taken by the researcher	Coding for themes

Figure 7. Ethnographic Research Process

Once interviews were transcribed, each was coded by the colors red, blue, and green. The colors were used to identify which participant stated "what" and which themes emerged. Memos were used in the transcription documents. Field notes and reflective notes were maintained in a separate Word document. Eventually, all documents were brought together to identify any emerging themes for the HH. The research findings primarily deal with the subjective self-identification for the research participants.

Summary

In this chapter, the research design and procedures of data collection were briefly explained. This was meant to provide background information of the research design and data collection process and procedures. Additional information can be found in Appendix 1, Appendix 2, and Appendix 3 for the inquisitive readers.

CHAPTER 4

ETHNOGRAPHIC DESCRIPTION OF THE HISPANIC HYBRID IDENTITY FOUND IN MIAMI-DADE

Introduction

Hispanics today form one of the fastest-growing ethnic minorities in the United States.[20] Numbering about 56.6 million in 2015,[21] they make up the largest minority in the nation, African Americans being the next largest. Although Hispanics have experienced less outright discrimination (except in Texas and New Mexico) than have African Americans, some sections of this group have lower economic and education levels than does the rest of the population of the United States.

The term Hispanic does not only refer to an ethnic description. It also has implications to native language and to cultural background. Within the group called Hispanics are peoples of diverse ethnic origins. There are African Americans and American Indians as well as individuals of purely European background whose families have lived in the Americas for generations. And, because of intermarriage, there are descendants who represent a combination of several origins. Hispanics do not necessarily regard themselves as a single group because their attachments are to their specific national origin. In the case of many Mexican Americans, the national origin is within the United States if their ancestors lived in the Southwest before the Mexican War.

Puerto Ricans enjoy a different status from other Hispanics in that they are citizens of the United States by birth, whether they were born in their homeland or in the United States. Puerto Ricans may therefore go back and forth between the island and the mainland without visas or passports. Mexicans, Cubans, and others must enter the country as immigrants with alien status and must apply for citizenship in the same way as do other immigrants.

---

[20] Jens Manuel Krogstad, "Key Facts about how the U.S. Hispanic Population is Changing," Pew Research Center, Washington D.C., September 8, 2016, https://www.pewresearch.org/fact-tank/2016/09/08/key-facts-about-how-the-u-s-hispanic-population-is-changing/.

[21] United States Census Bureau, *Facts for Features: Hispanic Heritage Month 2016,* CB16-FF.16, October 12, 2016, http://www.census.gov/newsroom/facts-for-features/2016/cb16-ff16.html.

Although there are Hispanics in most parts of the United States, some areas have especially large concentrations. Texas and California account for more than 50 percent of the total Hispanic population in the United States. About 60 percent of Cuban Hispanics reside in Florida, with the heaviest concentration in Miami-Dade County.[22]

Hispanics in Miami

In January 1959, Fidel Castro overthrew the Cuban dictatorship of Fulgencio Batista. Relations with the United States soon began to deteriorate. Castro confiscated property belonging to American companies, announced his intention of fomenting revolution throughout Latin America, and established close ties with the Soviet Union. In January 1961, President Eisenhower broke diplomatic relations with Cuba. Four months later, in the early months of President John F. Kennedy's administration, about 1,500 anti-Castro Cubans invaded the southwestern coast of Cuba at a place called the Bay of Pigs.[23] This invasion had been planned by the United States Central Intelligence Agency with the help of Cubans who hoped that Castro would be easily overthrown.

The Bay of Pigs invasion was a complete failure. But it did not end the hopes of Cubans in the United States that Castro's regime would be short-lived and that they would soon be able to return to their homeland. They came to the United States as refugees beginning in 1959; their exodus has not ceased.

The modern migration of Cubans to the United States began in 1959 as Castro's victory seemed imminent. Those who came to the United States were not the poorest segments of society, as had been the case with Mexicans and Puerto Ricans. They were members of the prosperous middle class: shop owners, businesspeople, and professionals who feared the consequences of a Castro takeover. The first Cubans to arrive were those who escaped. Later arrivals for the most part consisted of those allowed by the Cuban government to leave.

During the years 1961 through 1970, a total of 256,769[24] Cuban immigrants were admitted to the United States. The largest number to arrive in a single year during that decade was 99,312 in 1968. Another 270,000 came during the next decade. On April 4, 1980, Castro allowed the Peruvian Embassy in Havana to be opened to Cubans who wished to leave the island. Within a few days the number wishing to get away had grown to more than 10,000. Castro decided on April 20, to open the port of Mariel on Cuba's north coast for those who wanted to go to the United States. In the next five months

---

[22] R. A. Guisepi, and various authors, "Hispanic Americans," *History World International*, accessed March 28, 2019, http://history-world.org/hispanics.html.

[23] John F. Kennedy Presidential Library and Museum, "The Bay of Pigs," accessed March 28, 2019, https://www.jfklibrary.org/learn/about-jfk/jfk-in-history/the-bay-of-pigs.

[24] Caryn E. Neumann, "Cuban Immigrants," *Immigration to the United States*, accessed March 28, 2019, http://immigrationtounitedstates.org/453-cuban-immigrants.html.

about 123,000 new Cuban refugees landed in Florida. Among them were about 5,000 criminals and a larger number of persons who had been held as political prisoners.

The Refugee Act of 1980[25] drastically reduced the number of Cubans allowed into the country. President Carter therefore classified the "Marielitos" as entrants with their status pending. These new arrivals were unlike the previous Cuban immigrants in that they were mostly young, single, adult males. Only a very small number of them could speak any English, and their educational level was generally lower than that of previous arrivals. They arrived when the United States' economy was in a recession and finding sponsors or jobs for them was difficult. To accommodate these new aliens, President Carter opened processing centers at various military bases across the country.

The uncertain status of the Marielitos lasted until October 17, 1984, when Congress reenacted the Cuban Refugee Act of 1966. This restored the favorable status Cuban refugees had enjoyed before 1980 and allowed their processing to start within six weeks. By the end of 1985, most of them had received permanent residency status in the United States, which allowed them to apply for citizenship after five years.

Cuban Americans

By the early 1990s, there were well over one million Cuban Americans in the United States. They had come mostly as refugees, which distinguished them from the other large Hispanic groups. Because of their refugee status they were offered help from the federal government; other groups did not receive this. The Cuban Refugee Resettlement Program provided them with financial assistance and help in finding housing.

Cuban Americans live in most major cities in the United States. By far the largest settlement is in south Florida, and the second largest is in and around Union City, New Jersey. Other Hispanics have tended to disperse themselves around the country. Cubans, by contrast, continue to concentrate in south Florida, where about 60 percent of Cuban Americans lived by 1992. In contrast to urban Mexican Americans and Puerto Ricans, Cuban Americans are not concentrated in the ghetto neighborhoods of cities. Their prosperity has enabled them to move to the suburbs. Every part of Miami-Dade County, Florida, has some Cuban population.

---

[25] US Department of Health and Human Services, Administration for Children and Families, Office of Refugee Resettlement, The Refugee Act of 1980, Public Law 96-212, March 17, 1980, last reviewed May 15, 2019, accessed March 28, 2019, https://www.acf.hhs.gov/orr/resource/the-refugee-act.

Miami

Cubans succeeded in transforming southern Florida in much the same way that Mexican immigrants changed the border area of the United States and Mexico. Miami-Dade County's population is more than 40 percent Cuban.

As many Cubans prospered and left areas originally settled, that part of the city changed. Other Hispanics arrived to replace the departed Cubans, immigrants from Nicaragua, Colombia, El Salvador, and other Latin American countries. Within greater Miami, in 1990, there were more than 200,000 non-Cuban Hispanics, including the sizable Puerto Rican colony.

The Evolving Identity of Miami-Dade County

Normal cities grow because of the heritage that has been established through generations, mainly in the elite categories. Miami grew through the elites that were imported from other countries, thus transplanting the power brokers that were already there. Strategically, Miami is the only city in the Western hemisphere that has equal access to both North and South America. Within an air-flight radius of twenty-four hours lie all of the capitals, ports, and trade centers of North and South America. Economic thrust has come into Miami based on five factors:

1.	Cubans arrived in Miami at an opportune time when development was slowing down, thus allowing for a new economy to start.
2.	Miami was not as deeply established as other cities, therefore newcomers had ample opportunities to contribute and develop from within the city.
3.	The immigrants coming in had business expertise and international connections which facilitated trade further and faster.
4.	Miami was strategically located to be able to do work both domestically and internationally.
5.	The economy was fueled with international capital; a strong source of that was through drug trafficking.

Figure 8. Five Economic Factors that Shaped Miami[26]

There is evidence that suggests associating selective acculturation with greater transnational involvement, but also some limited evidence of downward assimilation associated with higher rates of sending financial assistance among some nationalities. The different ethnicities that live in Miami are not inter-dependent; rather they are more interethnic cohabitants

[26] Jan Nijman, *Miami: Mistress of the Americas* (Philadelphia: University of Pennsylvania Press, 2011), 94-116.

confined to the same space. A distinction needs to be made between selective acculturation and consonant acculturation. The former has a higher association with the culture of origin as it is immigration by choice. The latter does not have a high level of involvement as these immigrants have chosen to leave due to negative factors such as poverty, instability in government, war, or a poor financial infrastructure.[27] This thinking is foundational for the development of an ethnographic study.

Cultural development of the HH is impacted by three social factors which are represented in a status of sorts: locals, exiles, and mobiles. Locals are those who consider Miami to be their hometown, roughly 20% of the population. Exiles are those who find themselves in Miami because of political or economic necessity. They are generally in Miami waiting for political turmoil to change. Mobiles do not identify with Miami as their home and, like exiles, do not consider their stay in Miami permanent. Unlike exiles, mobiles have come to Miami by choice and they can leave by choice due to their affluence. Compared to other metropolitan areas, many of Miami's foreign immigrants belong to the upper income classes.

Despite the surface level challenges that are found in Miami, it is still in a unique way an emblematic representation of America's future. Cities will become more global, increasingly multicultural, and more transient. Urban cultures will be more fragmented, less localized, and urban elites will be increasingly care-free. Producer services and finance will continue to grow and spread. Air travel and technology will connect cities to the wider world, foreign dimensions connections will be more available, and trans-nationalism will be ever more the norm.[28]

Cultural Dimensions: Cuba, Colombia, Nicaragua, and the U.S.A.

To best understand the ethnographic profile of the HH, one must first understand the cultural and anthropological origins of the people being studied. In Miami, the three largest ethnic Hispanic populations represented are from Cuba, Nicaragua, and Colombia; see table below.

---

[27] Haller and Landolt.

[28] Nijman, *Miami,* 201-13.

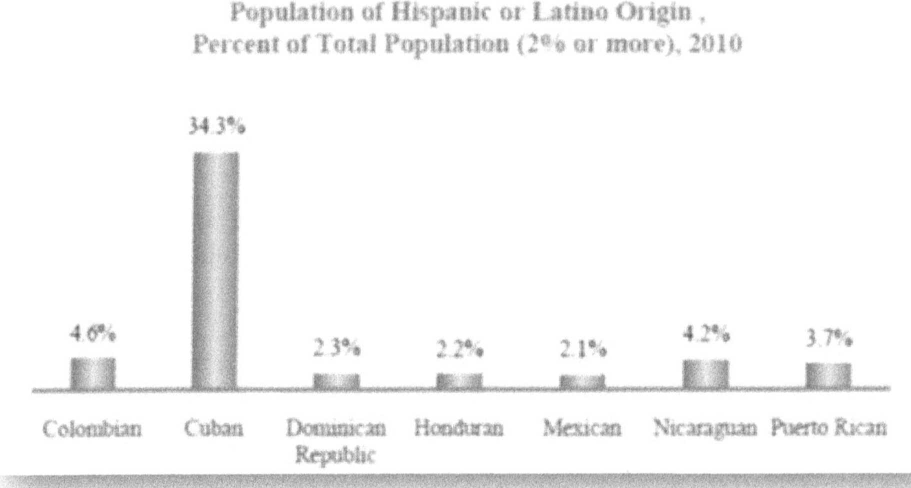

Figure 9. Hispanic Populations in Miami

Much has been written in the field of ethnography referring to the ethnicities mentioned above. Therefore, in this following section, each of the countries will be observed through the filter of Hofstede's Cultural Dimensions. The intent is to help distinguish the variances between the HH and Diaspora cultures that make it up. From these comparisons and the input from the research participants, the researcher will provide an ethnographic profile which will inform an initial Cultural Dimension for the HH. The five Cultural Dimensions used are: Power Distance, Individualism, Masculinity, Uncertainty Avoidance, and Pragmatism.[29]

The "Power Distance" dimension deals with the fact that all individuals in societies are not equal. It expresses the attitude of the culture towards these inequalities amongst all people.

"Collectivism vs. Individualism" refers to the degree of interdependence a society maintains among its members. It has to do with whether a people's self-image is defined in terms of individuals ("I") or groups ("We"). In an Individualist society, people are supposed to look after themselves and their direct family only. In a Collectivist society, people belong to "in groups" which take care of them in exchange for loyalty.

A high score in the "Masculinity vs. Femininity" dimension indicates that the society will be driven by competition, achievement, and success, with

---

[29] Hofstede Insights, *The Six Dimensions of National Culture*, accessed March 28, 2019, https://www.hofstede-insights.com/models/national-culture/. At the time of investigation and analysis, the Hofstede site comprised Five Dimensions of National Culture. Only five dimensions are included in the analysis and exposition.

success being defined by the "winner" or "best in field," which are considered "masculine." This is a value system that starts in early education and continues throughout organizational behavior. A low score on the dimension scale indicates that the dominant values in society are caring for others and quality of life, which is rated as "feminine." A feminine society is one where quality of life is the sign of success and standing out from the crowd is not admirable. The fundamental issue here is what motivates people; wanting to be the best (masculine) or liking what one does (feminine).

The dimension "Uncertainty Avoidance" has to do with the way a society deals with the fact that the future can never be known. Should one try to control the future or just let it happen? This ambiguity brings with it anxiety. Different cultures have learned to deal with anxiety in different ways. The extent to which the members of a culture feel threatened by ambiguous or unknown situations and have created beliefs and institutions that try to avoid these is reflected in the Uncertainty Avoidance Index score.

The "Pragmatism" dimension describes how every society has to maintain some connections to its own past while dealing with the challenges of the present and future, recognizing that societies prioritize these two existential goals differently. Normative societies, who score low on this dimension, prefer to maintain time-honored traditions and norms while viewing societal change with suspicion. Those with a culture which scores high, on the other hand, take a more pragmatic approach: they encourage thrift and efforts in modern education as a way to prepare for the future.

Cultural Dimensions: Cuba

Cuba has a very high Power Distance. This is due to the dictatorship established by Fidel Castro and his regime. Castro for years had, and his regime continues to, control everything from religion, property, economics, and all expression of industrial organizations. This form of power has been present through most of Cuba's history. From its beginning, Cuba has been under control of other leaders and nations, including the United States.

Being that Cuba has been and continues to be under rule as a Communist nation, it is considered to be a collectivist culture. People are forced to work together, knowing that cooperation is crucial. Cubans believe that the well-being of all citizens is important and are therefore okay with making personal sacrifices for the good of the country. Cuba is an isolated country, and citizens collectively share a pride in their country's independence.[30]

Cuba is considered a more feminine culture. Women have taken many strides forward in work and home life. Women now hold nearly 37% of the seats in parliament and men are also given the option of maternity leave. This

---

[30] David Gates et al., "A Taste of Salsa," Newsweek, January 19, 1998, 43, Academic Search Premier, EBSCO.

all began when Cuba signed the Convention on the Elimination of All Forms of Discrimination against Women. This brought about equality and integrity for women.[31]

As a country, Cuba falls more into the category of High Uncertainty Avoidance. This is perpetuated by the fact that Castro's dictatorship strictly enforces the set rules in hopes of eliminating any unwanted changes in the country's structure.

Cuba appears to have a more short-term orientation. Their people live life day to day with a relaxed view on structure. They also have not done much planning for the future economically or politically. Because of the nature of poverty, long-term investing is an impossibility there. Throughout history they have pushed away many economic allies, and their political system has been impetuously run by a dictator who did not leave a plan for his absence.

Cubans are considered to be a "present oriented" people. They tend to live in the moment and are in no hurry to get things done. They have never really been in control of their destiny so it is pointless and frustrating to focus too much on the future.[32]

Cubans view others in a combination of both good and bad. They believe that people's behaviors are a choice and that each makes decisions to do right or wrong. Religion is also split. Some are very religious thinking that all are good; some are Atheist and believe the opposite.[33] Cubans tend to be very subordinate by nature. They accept things as they are and take what they are given. They have for years simply accepted Castro and his dictatorship. It is clear that they disapprove this expression of government and its leadership; however, they have grown accustomed and have adapted to living within its confines.

Cubans are a "being" culture. Fidel Castro controls many aspects of their life and has limited the incentive for people to want to try to rise to the top.[34] They are also hierarchical in their social organization. Their government for years has been run by Castro. He has recently passed away and transferred power to his brother, Raul Castro. The hierarchy is also demonstrated within the home. The eldest male father is the loudest authority. The eldest female mother is the final authority.

---

[31] Malena Hinze, "The Revolutionary Role of Women in Cuba," *Liberation,* March 1, 2006, https://www.liberationnews.org/06-03-01-the-revolutionary-role-women-in-html/.
[32] C. Peter Ripley, Conversations with Cuba (Athens, GA: The University of Georgia Press, 1999).
[33] Emma Gobin and Geraldine Morel, "Ethnography and Religious Anthropology of Cuba: Historical and Biographical Landmarks," *Ateliers d'anthropologie* 38 (2013), https://doi.org/10.4000/ateliers.9447.
[34] Gobin and Morel.

Cultural Dimensions: Colombia

When the Colombian culture is filtered through the lens of the Hofstede Cultural Dimensions Model,[35] one can arrive at an accurate overview of the drivers of its culture, relative to other world cultures. Colombia scores high on the Power Distance (PDI) scale. They are a society that believes that inequalities amongst people are a simple fact of life. This inequality is accepted in all layers of society. A similar phenomenon can be observed among business leaders and among the highest positions in government.

Colombians scored among the lowest individualistic scores in this category. They are one of the more collectivistic cultures in the world, beaten only by Ecuador, Panama, and Guatemala. Since the Colombians are a highly collectivistic people, belonging to an in-group and aligning one's self with that group's opinion is very important. Combined with the high scores in PDI, this group will often identify strongly with class distinctions. Loyalty to such groups is paramount and often it is through "cooperative" groups that people obtain privileges and benefits which are not to be found in other cultures. At the same time, conflict is avoided in order to maintain group harmony and to save face.

Relationships are more important than attending to the task at hand, and when a group of people holds an opinion on an issue, they will be joined by all who feel part of that group. Colombians will often go out of their way to help you if they feel there is enough attention given to developing a relationship, or if they perceive an "in-group" connection of some sort, regardless of how thin. However, those perceived as "outsiders" can easily be excluded or considered as "enemies." The preferred communication style is context-rich, so public speeches and written documents are usually extensive and elaborate.

The Colombian culture is considered to be masculine. It is highly success oriented and driven. Colombians are competitive and status-oriented, yet collectivistic rather than individualistic. This means that competition is directed towards members of other groups or social classes, not towards those who are perceived as members of one's own in-group. People seek membership in groups which give them status and rewards linked to performance, but they often sacrifice leisure against work, as long as this is supported by group membership and by power holders.

Colombian culture scored high in the area of uncertainty avoidance. Collectively, they are seeking mechanisms to avoid ambiguity. Emotions are openly expressed; there are extensive rules for everything and social conservatism enjoys quite a following. This is also reflected in religion, which is respected, followed by many and conservative. Rules are not necessarily followed, however, this depends on the in-group's opinion, on whether the

---

[35] Hofstede Insights, *Colombia Cultural Dimension*, accessed March 28, 2019, https://www.hofstede-insights.com/country/colombia/.

group feels the rules are applicable to their members and it is contingent, ultimately, on the decision of power holders, who make their own rules. In work terms this results in detailed planning that may not necessarily be followed in practice.

The combination of high UAI with the scores on the previous dimensions means that it is difficult to change the status quo, unless a figure of authority is able to amass a large group of people and lead them towards change.

With a low score in pragmatism, the Colombian culture is classified as normative. People in such societies have a strong concern with establishing the absolute Truth; they are normative in their thinking. They exhibit great respect for traditions, a relatively small propensity to save for the future, and a focus on achieving quick results.

Cultural Dimensions: Nicaragua

The average PDI for all Latin American countries is 70 out of 100.[36] While Nicaragua is considered a developing country, it is still in its infant stages of becoming a stable, independently functioning nation. While some argue that the influence of Western cultures in Nicaragua is generating a paradigm shift toward a lower power distance position, the nation's current cultural makeup indicates a relatively high power distance level. High power distance would suggest an important emphasis in the Nicaraguan society on a citizen's power, wealth, and the status or level of separation achieved through these means. Inequality is accepted as a norm in this culture and subordinates know their "place" in an organization or society. In Nicaragua, the less powerful are comfortable with inequality, and there is a considerable dependence of subordinates on bosses.

Given the cultural similarity between Nicaragua and Costa Rica (as well as the majority of Latin American cultures) in the construction of family and the value of group association, Nicaragua can be justly compared to the position of its neighbor, Costa Rica, on the individualism versus collectivism dimension. Costa Rica received a score of 15 and ranked 67th in a study of 74 regions.[37] Nicaragua is considered an exceedingly collectivist country and is very different than the United States, which ranked as the world's most individualistic country. This high collectivism in Nicaragua indicates that in its society, the "power of the group" and the mutual dependence relationship of people with a group is extremely important. One's membership in an "in-group" is the primary source of personal identity and protection through life.

To correctly understand the Masculinity versus Femininity dimension, one must be able to distinguish the difference between "sex roles," which are the

---

[36] S. Montenegro, "Nicaragua's Sexual Culture: A Loveless Legacy," *Revista Envio* 240 (July 2001), retrieved October 25, 2009, http://www.envio.org.ni/articulo/1515.

[37] Hofstede Insights, *Costa Rica Cultural Dimension*, accessed March 28, 2019, https://www.hofstede-insights.com/country/costa-rica/.

behaviors that denote a biological distinction between men and women, and "gender roles," which are the masculine and feminine behaviors men and women are culturally expected to play in society. Nicaragua, originally an indigenous culture, found gender models growing increasingly complex as it evolved into a multiethnic society throughout its history. For many years, two separate social formations coexisted in Nicaragua: a Spanish dominated culture on the Pacific side (*Mestizos*) and a culture influenced by British colonization on the Caribbean side. The reason Nicaragua so strongly identifies as masculine in this dimension involves the history of the Spanish dominated *Mestizo* culture. The *Mestizo* group emerged as a result of the Spanish conquest, with the Spanish mass raping the indigenous women during land occupations, forming a new ethnic group.

A new language, religion, and social order replaced the original indigenous culture, and the population demographics became increasingly complex. From the very start, "two republics were established, one for the Spanish and one for the natives. The state directed and protected the Spanish republic, while the natives worked and obeyed."[38] To avoid discrimination and the levies imposed on the natives, many of the *Mestizo* children tried (or were forced by their mothers) to break any kinship tie to the indigenous world, leading to the *Mestizos* becoming more Hispanic and therefore masculine, negating their indigenous origins and maternal culture. "The results of this psychic operation can still be seen today in Nicaragua's machismo with the violent humiliation of women and equally violent affirmation of the father."[39]

Nicaragua still operates on a day-to-day society cultural model that perceives women as subordinate to men. This model includes the stereotype that "women are exclusively responsible for caring for the children and doing other domestic tasks."[40] Although some progress has been made in attempting to change this model, families are nevertheless inherently unequal, "characterized still by paternal irresponsibility, domestic violence, and a sharp restriction on women's time ..."[41]

In Hofstedes' 2004 IBM study, all Latin American countries scored high in uncertainty avoidance.[42] Nicaragua, when aligned with similar Latin American cultures, likely ranks in the 17-22 percentiles, indicating relatively high uncertainty avoidance, much higher than the United States, which ranked 62. This high UAI indicates comparatively high anxiety levels in the Nicaraguan society. Nicaraguans are quite uncomfortable with ambiguity in all situations. The Nicaraguan culture, having this characteristic discomfort with the unknown, falls in line with the Hofstedes' observations in that its members do

---

[38] Montenegro.
[39] Montenegro.
[40] Montenegro.
[41] Montenegro.
[42] G. Hofstede and G. J. Hofstede, *Cultures and Organizations: Software of the Mind* (New York, NY: McGraw-Hill, 2004).

not feel comfortable letting children independently determine their own future. The researcher married an HH with a Nicaraguan background and can personally attest to this cultural reality. Instead of allowing children to decide, they developed the "*Compadrazgo*" system for their children with the sole purpose of providing an affluent liaison that can influence or help the child in the future by building a system of personal loyalties and connections. The previously discussed work responsibilities of young children characteristic of Nicaraguan culture also demonstrate high UAI tendency, in that families are very concerned with money and financial situations.[43] According to UNICEF, the net percentage of children attending primary school is only 73%, a consequence of the widespread child labor that prevents many children from completing primary school.[44]

As expected with a developing country in a constant state of revolution and change, Nicaragua is very short-term oriented. Only recently with the influence of Western-based assistance organizations has Nicaragua expressed any long-term oriented ideas, goals, or practices. At the time of this writing, the Ortega led, leftist-government, has exhausted the resources of the people, has raised taxes on all, removed benefits for the elderly because of an exhaustion to their social security, and has changed the constitution in order to have Ortega's wife as the current Vice-President. In April of 2018, a civil protest began among university students which has now become a national movement. The government has mobilized its national guard to address the protests and to use force as necessary.

Upon cross-examination of the Hofstedes' dimensions, it is easily seen with few exceptions that masculine, collectivist societies identify more fluidly with short-term orientation. One example of short-term orientation in Nicaraguan families deals with the treatment of children. While the young are an integral part of the family as contributing members, they are also cherished and valued simply as children.

Cultural Dimensions: U.S.A.

In the U.S.A., the ideology is that everybody is unique. This implies that we are all unequal, because all are unique. One of the most salient aspects of inequality is the degree of power each person exerts or can exert over other persons. Because of such varying degree, the U.S.A. has a low registered power distance.

The fairly low score on PDI, in combination with one of the

---

[43] University Center for International Studies [UCIS] (2004). "Family Life in Nicaragua: Illuminations: Cultural Formations of the Americas," 1, 1-2, retrieved September 28, 2009, accessed March 28, 2019. http://www.ucis.pitt.edu/clas/nicaragua_proj/society/Family/Soc-familylife.pdf.

[44] UNICEF (2006), UNICEF Nicaragua, *United for Children*, retrieved November 8, 2009, accessed March 28, 2019, http://www.unicef.org/index.php.

most individualistic cultures in the world has many expressions.[45] The American premise of "liberty and justice for all" is one of them. This is evidenced by an explicit emphasis on equal rights in all aspects of American society and government. Within American organizations, hierarchy is established for convenience, superiors are accessible, and managers rely on individual employees and teams for their expertise.

Society is loosely-knit in which the expectation is that people look after themselves and their immediate families only and should not rely (too much) on authorities for support. There is also a high degree of geographical mobility in the United States. Americans are the best "joiners" in the world; however, it is often difficult, especially among men, to develop deep friendships. Americans are accustomed to doing business or interacting with people they don't know well. Consequently, Americans are not shy about approaching their prospective counterparts in order to obtain or seek information. In the business world, employees are expected to be self-reliant and display initiative. Also, within the exchange-based world of work we see that hiring, promotion, and decisions are based on merit or evidence of what one has done or can do.

The score of the U.S.A. on Masculinity is high and this can be seen in the typical American behavioral patterns. This can be explained by the combination of a high Masculinity drive together with the most individualistic drive in the world. In other words, Americans show their masculine drive individually.

This combination reflects itself from education to employment. In school, work, and play, there are shared values that people should "strive to be the best they can be" and that "the winner takes all." As a result, Americans will tend to display and talk freely about their "successes" and achievements in life. Being successful per se is not the great motivator in American society, but being able to show one's successes is.

Typically, Americans "live to work" so that they can obtain monetary rewards and as a consequence attain higher status based on how good one can be. Many white-collar workers will move to a higher end community after each and every substantial promotion. Rising inequality is endangering democracy, because a widening gap among the classes may slowly push Power Distance up and Individualism down. This has been one of the major factors in previous years and in the 2016 Presidential Election.

The U.S.A. scores below average on the Uncertainty Avoidance dimension. The perceived context in which Americans find themselves will impact their behavior more than if the culture would have either scored higher or lower. This creates space for a fair degree of acceptance for new ideas, innovative products, and a willingness to try something new or different, whether it

---

45 Hofstede Insights, *United States Cultural Dimension,* accessed March 28, 2019, https://www.hofstede-insights.com/country/the-usa/.

pertains to technology, business practices, or food. Americans tend to be more tolerant of ideas or opinions from anyone and allow the freedom of expression. At the same time, Americans do not require a lot of rules and are less emotionally expressive than higher-scoring cultures. Because of global instability and acts of terrorism (domestic and international), this has created much fear in the American society culminating in the efforts of government to monitor everyone through the federal security organizations.

The United States scores normative on the fifth dimension with a low score. This is because Americans are prone to analyze new information to validate whether it is true or false. This cultural expression does not make most Americans pragmatic, and this is not to be confused with the fact that Americans are very functional, being reflected by the "can-do" mentality. Because of the polarization mentioned, this dimension is strengthened by the fact that many Americans have very strong ideas about what is "good" and "evil." Because American businesses measure their performance on a short-term basis, with profit and loss statements being issued on a quarterly basis, this also drives individuals to strive for quick results within the work place.

Cultural Dimensions of the HH

One can imagine the difficulty in trying to properly gauge the HH of Miami. With the blending of the ethnicities mentioned above, the outcome is truly unique. In the following section, the researcher develops a Cultural Dimension of the HH from the research findings above along with his emic perspective as G1.5 who has lived in Miami the majority of his life, thirty-five years plus. When one considers the four countries above, some consistencies in the ethnic groups arise which largely explain how many of the G2s and HHs operate today.

In all the ethnic groups observed, the PDI ranked very high. The only one that ranked low was that of U.S.A. Among the HH, one finds that among peer relationships, usually the social ones, HH's are very similar to the rest of the U.S.A. They experience freedom in speaking and feedback. Within the home of an HH, there still remains a high Power Distance from elder to youth, parent to child. Because of ethnic upbringing and values, the home is still the primary point of influence in the life of an HH, whether child or adult. In places of work, there is a clear Power Distance between employer and employee. The PDI for the HHs ranks fairly high.

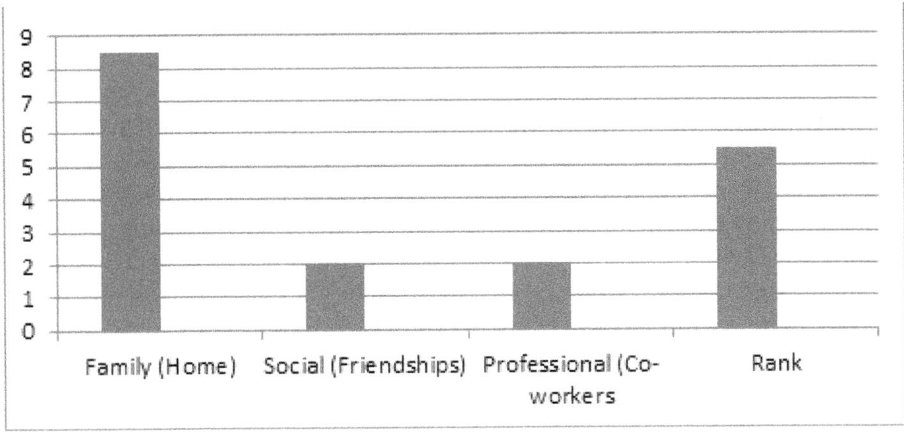

Figure 10. Power Distance Hispanic Hybrid

The HHs who were interviewed indicated a higher score on the Collective Dimension. As noted above, each Hispanic ethnicity scored on the higher end of the collective scale. Cubans were high in collectivism because of their governmental structures. Colombians were high in collectivism because of their desire to belong to a group for status. Nicaraguans were high in collectivism because of their suppression and desire to exercise group power. Without doubt, these factors have continued to impact the rearing of children, even though they were born and raised in the U.S.A. However, the host culture has had an impact on the HH and his take on collectivism. For HHs who become more individualistic, it is not uncommon for them to marry outside of the Hispanic culture, though this does not occur frequently yet. Often times, if this happens, the HH is likely to move out of Miami into a more "American" culture. When one considers the areas of family, professionalism, and social relationships, the HH has some unique reasons for their scores.

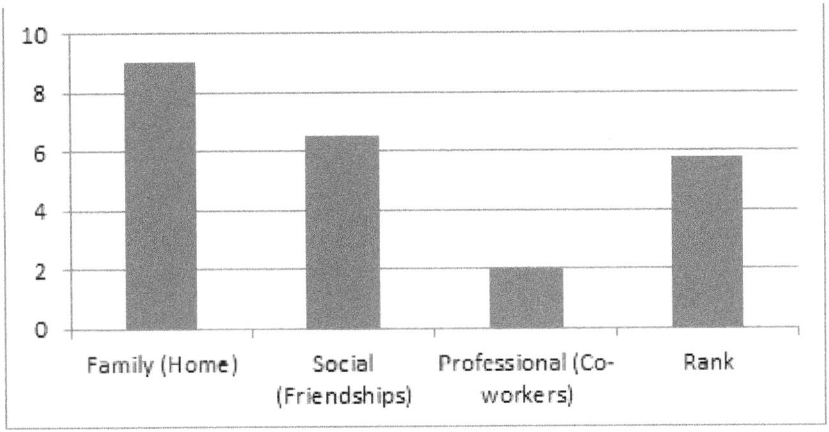

Figure 11. Collectivism Hispanic Hybrid

In the area of family, there is no surprise that the HH would rank high as collective. Based on the researcher's perspective, the family structure in any Hispanic culture is central and core. In the area of social relationships, there is also a high collectivist rank. This is due in part to the desire to be accepted socially in Miami. Social acceptance in Miami is perceived to be a symbol of some status. Because of the outgoing nature of the culture, involvement with others is important. This matters as one would not want to be perceived socially awkward or taboo. In the area of work, there is a high score as an individual. Since there is potential to move up in employment and income, HHs seek to do so, not in order to help family that may remain in their home country, rather for their own self benefit, preservation, and familial benefit (those in Miami).

Of all of the Hispanic countries in this study, Cuba is the only one with a score that lends itself to be Feminine. The Cuban government may be the most progressive of all, having strong women leadership in place. This in turn has impacted the home and how it operates. Most Cuban homes, even in Miami, are led by the matriarch. The other Hispanic countries and the U.S.A. ranked high in terms of masculinity.

Colombia is highly driven by success and social status. Nicaragua's history of Spanish rule and conquering lead them to be influenced by Western European masculinity. The U.S.A.'s appeal to drive and to win leads them to be high on the masculinity scale as well.

While Cubans are by far the highest population group of the research participants, this is one of the categories where the host culture and other Hispanic cultures have influenced the larger towards change. Those initial waves of Cuban migration in the 1960s and 1980s were regularly among the educated, wealthy, and mobile. Because of the opportunities afforded to them in the U.S.A., a cultural shift occurred. Today, Miami thrives because of the Hispanic commerce, education, wealth, and status, much of it Cuban in origin, led by men.

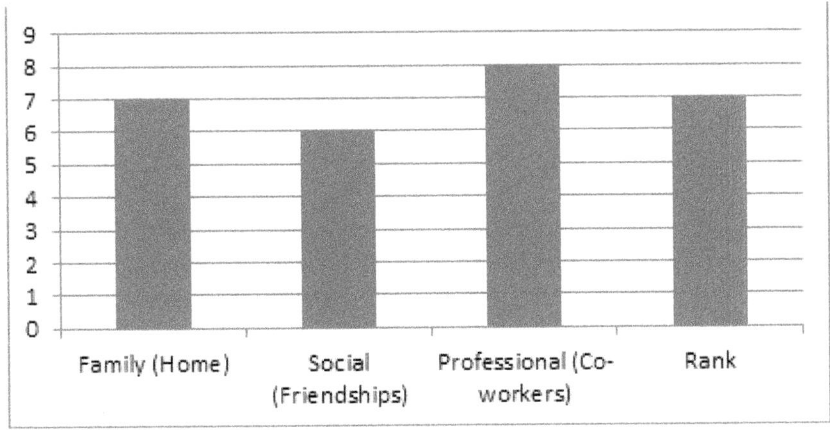

Figure 12. Masculinity Hispanic Hybrid

This high rank in masculinity is one of the main explanations as to why Miami still sounds and behaves like a Latin American city in the U.S.A. The culture has not allowed itself to be dominated by another. It is not likely to change towards assimilation to host culture any time soon. Conversely, the HH culture has learned how to operate within the host culture and to make the most of the opportunities that are afforded to them. The HH perceive this as the best of both worlds.

The Hispanics in this study all had high ranks in the area of uncertainty. This is due mainly to combinations of instable government, financial markets, and corrupt systems. HHs differ from their parents and grandparents in the scheme of uncertainty. Because they were not born or raised in their family's country of origin, their perception is limited only to what they know. In Miami, the HHs benefit from the perceived safety and security that is offered in the U.S.A. A more stable government, economy, healthcare system, international environment, and education are all part of the appeal of living in Miami. The concerns that the HH have differ from parents. Primary concerns that the HH have are the cost of living, future employment opportunities, and preservation of the family.

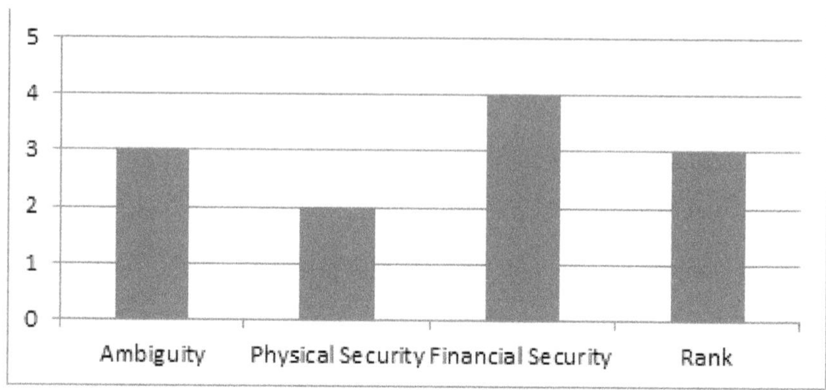

Figure 13. Uncertainty Avoidance Hispanic Hybrid

Every culture in the area of pragmatism, including the U.S.A., scored very low. In Cuba, due to the governmental structure and poverty, nothing is guaranteed. Long term planning is pointless. Colombian culture is strong on tradition. Doing things the same way over and over is part of that culture's ethos. There is little need to plan because change is unlikely. Nicaraguans have been victims of governmental coups and societal revolutions. Change is a constant there. Planning for the long term has also been seen as irrelevant. Americans also operate out of short-term perspective as they seek to make the most out of every moment, now. This is most notably seen in athletics, education, and finances as each one can be measured in quick increments of time and deemed successful or not.

For the HH, this short-term approach seems to hold true. Among research participants, there was little mention about the future, other than the desire to preserve and better the family. This may be in part because of the blending mentioned above. The "American dream" is there for the HH to take. With enough work today, one can have what they want today. Incomes are much greater today than when the initial waves of immigrants arrived in Miami. Many HH have more money today than their parents ever will. All of the research participants articulated growing up in middle to middle upper standards of living compared to their parents and their peers. As adults, the HH will work to improve and enjoy their better status today.

The HH is able to move up economically and socially because there are lower risks and higher opportunities of return for them. While their parents and grandparents sought simply to "make it," the HH seeks to make it bigger and better in the name of family.

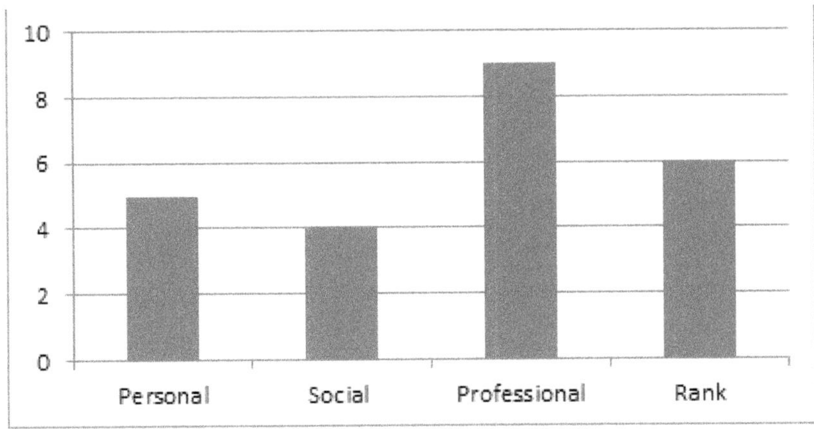

Figure 14. Pragmatism Hispanic Hybrid

In light of the Cultural Dimensions of the HH, the following section will be the initial ethnography of the HH.

Summary

In this chapter, research findings have been presented in terms of ethnographic description of the Hispanic hybrid identity found in Miami-Date County. The background is therefore provided to discuss Hispanic hybrids in terms of relational and cultural identity in chapter five.

CHAPTER 5

HISPANIC HYBRIDS: RELATIONAL AND CULTURAL IDENTITIES

Introduction

Along with new immigration, the G1.5 and G2 generation Hispanics are immigrant children. They grow up in the U.S.A. and become more distant from their home culture, yet not completely integrated into what is recognized as typical North American culture. A result is the blending of cultures that led towards the emergence of an identity of Hispanic Hybridity.[46] It was the desire of the researcher to develop an ethnographic understanding of the "in between" generations that have been and are currently emerging. The following diagram illustrates various points of contact which leads to the emergence and "blooming" of Hispanic hybrids in Miami-Dade with the three largest populations of Hispanic immigrants as base for this ethnographic study.

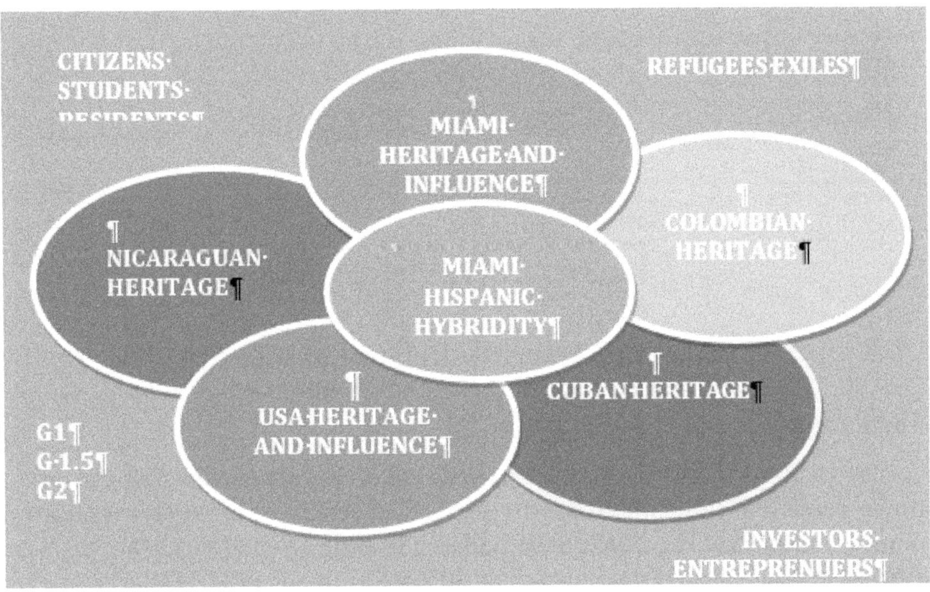

Figure 15. Dimensions of the Hispanic Hybrid

[46] Kraidy, 5.

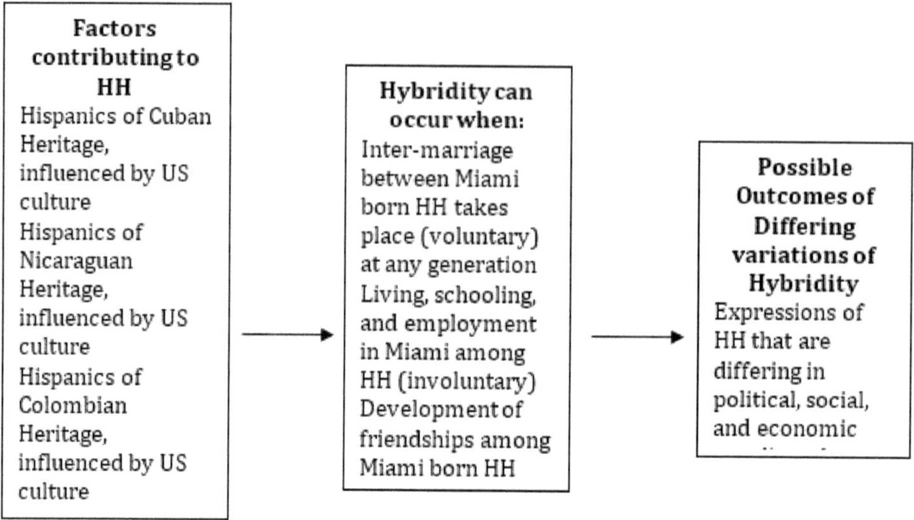

Figure 16. Hybridity Development of Hispanic Hybrid

Along with factors that contribute to ethnic identity, Hybridity also occurs when the fusion of differing ethnic generations occurs as indicated below.

Figure 17. Hybridity Spectrum

Hispanic Hybrids: Relational Identity

The Family

The Hispanic family in Miami has very clear characteristics that can, at times, seem like contradictions. On the surface level, the family structure is a monogamous one. The Cultural Dimension finding seems to indicate the same. However, when a closer look is taken into the home of a HH in Miami, one may be surprised to know that it is often the mother that carries the greatest amount of power in the decision-making process. Every single one of the research participants stated that in the day to day functions of the home and structural order, the mother assumes primary responsibility in this area.

This is most easily noted when it comes to the rearing of G2 and HH children, family planning. It is not uncommon for the father to passively watch as the family is developed around him and for him not to get involved in matters of authority until after it's too late or when the mother has "lost" control of the situation. The mother's position in the home is not to be taken as an absence of the father or a lack of care by the father. The father's role is usually perceived as the primary income winner and financial supporter of the home. According to our research participants, this practice was found to be true in every expression of Hispanic, G1–HH.

The role of family continues to be essential for the HH. A significant part of their individual and collective identity is found and formed in the context of family. In a presentation to the University of Houston–Clear Lake, it was noted that the word *FAMILY* carries with it a sense of unity not only among the nuclear family, but among the extended family as well.[47] The definition of success is critical to understanding the family structure. G1 homes view success not in terms of individual, rather in terms of family betterment. Often times, this is the primary reason why the family came to the U.S.A.: there was a greater opportunity for the family. All HH research participants could point to a moment when an initial patriarch or matriarch made the sacrifice to come and start over for the betterment of the home.

G2s become more individualistic in terms of success because of the types of opportunities that are presented to them and the lack of struggle that they have had to face in order to receive them. Unlike their parents, many G2s have not had to face nor overcome any significant obstacles to gain education, healthcare, or even employment. This can be likened unto the baby boomer generation and the generation before them. In terms of success, G2s are more often similar to a traditionally North American perspective of success: i.e. better education, better employment, bigger home, etc.: the American Dream. This is often the metric that determines who "made it." In the Hispanic home, a parent's success is measured on how they were able to raise their children and what kinds of opportunities where they able to provide for them.

For the HH, the family is still the central point of focus of priority and value. The difference is found in the inter-ethnic blending that occurs. Most G1 and G2 homes tend to marry persons of shared ethnic culture and country. The HH of Miami, while they are marrying other Hispanics, are not necessarily marrying Hispanics from the same country. This has posed some challenges on HH families as they seek to develop new norms and patterns for this newest expression of family.

Among the research participants, it was noted that one culture usually became more dominant than the other. No HH home was truly fifty-fifty in their expression. Food, some tradition, and family celebrations were normally preserved. In the everyday life, however, the HH home tended to lean in the direction of one culture more than another. The Cuban culture was normally

[47] Laurie Weaver and Judith Marquez, "Characteristics of Hispanic Families," (presentation, University of Houston – Clear Lake, n.d.).

the dominant culture in HH homes where Cuban HHs had married HHs of other cultures.

Proximity and distance among family was also affected in HH homes. Proximity to the nuclear family and grandparents (if they are in Miami) was still present. Beyond that, a distance begins to occur in the HH homes. One of the indicators to this happening was the size of family with so many that are family by marriage. At this point, family is redefined. There is a hesitation to welcoming new family as true family because of different ethnic background and socio-economic statuses. Family formation and identification for that HH, at the point of marriage can be recognized as association by affinity and preference. Among the HH research participants who are mobile and local, the expression of family shared the same ethnic and socio-economic backgrounds. The Hispanic ethnicity and the socio-economics served as a bridging factor. For those of exile descendants, the blending of culture led to an acculturation to the host culture which in this case is not the U.S.A., but that of Miami.

The redefinition of family impacts the treatment of biological and communal family. When it comes to doing "good" and "taking care of the family," the general response of the HH towards family and close friends is socially expected. Having positive will towards others is normal among many, with reservations. There is a high sense of distrust towards many. Many in the research articulated a kinship towards selected friends and family that is not extended to all. One participant used the term "Framily" to describe this. This is when friends become the new family of the HH. Miami has a reputation for being an unfriendly place because many living within proximity of each other do not relate to others socially very often, unless there is an emergency. This is actually a courtesy extended to each other as it maintains security among the Hispanics living in Miami. For the HH, minding one's own business is what keeps the social order intact among a people that may be in the U.S.A. illegally or potentially harboring those that are in the U.S.A. illegally.

Relationships at Home

As mentioned above, it is common for the man to be the sole provider of income for the home. However, in G2 and HH homes, women often work full time jobs along with their male counterparts besides maintaining many of the household responsibilities. Among HH males, there is a shift that is indicating more regular involvement in the life of the family as a response to the absence of the father in a G1 and at times G2 home.

G2s normally maintain their heritage with a solid bicultural framework. They are able to operate in their culture of origin and in a North American culture. Their children, the HH, strongly identify as more "American" than Hispanic. They were born, raised, and educated in the U.S.A. While Miami is still Miami, there is a solidarity in identifying with the rest of the country in their cultural heritage and roots. There is less working knowledge of home country and history. Each participant has emotional ties to their country because of their parents and their family's experience, not because of their own personal experience. One participant stated that he has "borrowed feelings and emotions" from his parents toward his family's country of origin while strongly holding that "I am American too."

This sentiment, however, is very inconsistent in HH rationale. Recently, at the time of this writing, the 2018 World Cup took place in Russia. While G1s and G2s were openly sharing their support for home teams (the teams which represented their home countries), not the U.S.A. The HH was also quite present in its support. In light of being "American too," one could assume that the HH would mainly support Team U.S.A., the team which represents their country of birth and the only nation they have ever experienced. This was not the case. Among all male participants, each of them articulated favorable support to the team which represented their family's country of origin first, then Team U.S.A. At times, the HH is very pro-Hispanic origin, then pro-U.S.A. This is the pattern for events like the last Olympic Games, the previous World Cup, current national political races, and international conflicts. The local identity as a Hispanic for an HH is still stronger than the national identity in certain areas of life. As Figure 1 illustrates (chapter 2), the HH is the result of immigration patterns, chain migration, and illegal migration, of the mobiles and exiles from G1 to today. As a result, the HH in Miami does not fully understand what it means to be American, in this sense of the host culture, unless they leave Miami, experience life "out there" and eventually acculturate.

Family Ties to Home

Family ties to the original culture are mainly preserved thru G1 relationships. The G1s were born and some raised among family back "home." While the G2 family may know the family back "home" (cousins, uncles, aunts, etc.), to the HH, the extended family in their country of origin is normally distant family at best. They did not grow up together nor do they have any shared experiences with this part of their family. The G1, grandmother/grandfather/parents, are often the ones that make the phone calls or go back to visit. They are the ones with the existing relationship with the extended family in their country of origin. The G2 tends to be distant and disconnected from the original family. After the G1 generation passes away, family ties if any, will be minimal or cease to exist.

For the HH, their contact with the family back "home" is minimal. There were some research participants who maintained some connection to their home country. Their primary reason to stay connected to family and travel back was to maintain culture, language, business, international influence for themselves and for their children. The HHs that were more mobile, traveling back and forth, tended to be more bilingual and bicultural. Part of their identity was formed and preserved through language, travel, and relational proximity. This represented a very small portion of the HH research participants.

The exiles tended to stay in greater contact with family from back home. This is due to a greater shared identity in economic and legal standing with their home family. The children of exiles, G1.5s and G2s, parents of HHs, did not seem to maintain much contact with family in their home countries. HHs born to exiles tend to lose relationships with their extended families since they never interacted with them; they do not have the means. To HH from exile families, their family in another country remains exactly that, distant and not likely to be understood. Thus, HHs of exiles demonstrated a greater cultural identity with other HHs in Miami. They also spoke mainly English, in some cases, English only. Some HH research participants understood both English and Spanish.

New Found Family

The formation of the "new family" was demonstrated to be essential to G1s and G2s if they stayed in Miami. Each of these generations, upon their arrival, sought out others who shared in their experience of struggle and opportunity. They enclaved together to establish new communities such as Little Havana (West of City of Miami), Little Managua (Sweet Water), and Little Colombia (Doral). Because of its diversity, G1s and G2s have been able to find others of similar culture and experience. The development of these new neighborhoods led to the rise of the new family.

Most easily noticed, the formation of the new family is celebrated publicly via country specific festivals, carnivals, and even holidays of their home countries. Because of the continual flow of new immigration into Miami, the memory of "home" is always fresh on the minds of the city. While there are no hard numbers, current estimations on the number of undocumented immigrants, G1-G2, is well over 725,000 in the state of Florida, of which more than half reside in Miami Dade County.[48] The outcome of this immigration since the 1960's until today is the expression of the new family. Communities emerge because of shared ethnic and linguistic backgrounds. This close-knit network of relationships is what comprises the new family. A close family friend becomes the new *"tio/tia"* (uncle/aunt) and even new *"primo/a"* (cousin). Each of the research participants mentioned their own expression of a "family" member who is not related by blood, rather through relationship and proximity.

For the HH, the "new family" is made up of the nuclear family and extremely close relationships. One of the research participants used the word "Framily" to describe their experience with the development of their new

---

[48] Patricia Mazzei, "South Florida ranks No. 5 in undocumented immigrant population, study finds," *Miami Herald*, February 2, 2017, https://www.miamiherald.com/news/politics-government/article131785114.html.

family. This new family, this extended family is often determined by those of similar standings in education and socio-economics. Shared ethnic culture is not as important to the HH. A new culture is emerging that the HH identifies with most while still holding on to some of the home culture. The new family is defined more by how one identifies himself from position first, then an ethnic culture. In real time, no HH would ever state "I am a poor or wealthy Nicaraguan." The position would always be stated as a person who's a Nicaraguan-American. Actions, language, and behavior would quickly distinguish the HH culturally in terms of education and socio-economics.

Marriage

For G1s, marriage occurred in their home country and is maintained to that person. For G2s, marriage is often blended across language and cultural lines. While G2s often maintain their home culture, they typically find their spouse in Miami. Thus, it is common for G2s to marry those from different Latin American countries, North American Anglos, and not generally among African Americans or ethnicities of dark skin. When asking research participants about matters of race and integration of different races, this was an area where almost all of them indicated a fair amount of racism among their grandparents and parents; G1s and G2s. Even choosing to marry Hispanics who are dark skinned was a matter of concern. "Hay que preserver la raza," we must preserve the race. This sentiment and idea were held by the majority of parents and grandparents of the HH.

Foreigners are easily received into Miami because of the established diversity. However, entering the family can be challenging. The G1 can often be seen as racist, even against other Latin Americans; it all depends on their country of origin or skin color. Living in Miami is simple for foreigners. The challenge begins when a G2 and HH begin to integrate themselves romantically (dating/marriage) with others of different cultures. Among the HH, discrimination exists around color and it includes issues of economics and education. Tension also exists in the integration of North Americans into Hispanic family environments, though less than if a Hispanic were to marry a person with darker skin.

As far as picking a mate, about half of the research participants married a person of their same cultural background and ethnicity. For many of them, this was important. There are additional factors that seem to link differing ethnicities together. The two that arose often in the research are socio-economics and education. Wealth, enterprise, and intellect are factors that matter to the HH and their decision-making process about future spouses. The research also demonstrated that HHs of the same ethnicity yet different socio-economic status were not likely to be together. HHs of mobile and exile homes did not seem to be with each other.

A shift that has occurred among G1s and G2s is that of the matter of divorce: it is a choice. In former times back "home," although marriage may not have gone well, the thought process was to preserve the marriage for the wellbeing of the children and the home. Today, it's not like that. Half of the research participants indicated that they came from divorced homes. Divorce is rapidly affecting the Hispanic home, G1 women in particular. Their understanding of the laws and freedoms provided in the United States has impacted their views and actions. The divorce rate among Hispanics, particularly G1s has risen to over 68% in 2009.49 Marriage is no longer held to be a lifelong commitment once Hispanics arrive and settle in Miami.

One of the primary causes of divorce among Hispanics is infidelity. In 2003, the illegitimacy rate for children born to Hispanic G2 mothers was 45 percent, nearly double the white rate. Between 1980 and 2003, the illegitimacy rate for Hispanics increased by 91 percent.50 Hispanic women accounted for 20 percent of abortions in America in 2002, and were 2.7 times more likely than whites to end a pregnancy in this manner.51 According to a 2001 study based on older data, 34 percent of G2 women's first marriages ended in divorce within ten years; the figure for white women was 32 percent.52

HH children are coming from incomplete families or blended families. This trend is seen in mobiles, locals, and exiles. Socio-economics or education does not seem to impact the divorce rate among G1s, G2s, and older HHs.

For mobiles, the divorce seems to occur mainly because of infidelity. For exiles, it is happening due to separation and distance. As mentioned above, Miami's data on families is posing a unique challenge. As families break up and remarriage occurs, the potential for HH process continues to expand.

Marriage Rites and Rules

The Hispanic male, G1 and G2 males particularly, is viewed as having a *"machista"* type of attitude. This means that the man goes to work and provides economically for the home. It is his responsibility and duty to provide financial gain for the home. Conversely, for G1 and G2 women, their role is to care for the home and to raise the children. Women in G1 and some G2 relationships are coming from countries where their perceived status was higher than a servant though functioned in similar roles. This varies some

---

[49] Florida Vital Statistics of Marriage and Divorce, 2009, http://www.vitalstats@flheath.gov/

[50] Health, United States, 2005, 133.

[51] Alan Guttmacher Institute, "Abortion in Women's Lives" (Washington, DC: AGI, 2006), 20. Rates for Hispanics and whites were determined by comparing the percentages of total abortions accounted for by white and Hispanic women with their percentages of the total population. Population data from "Table 4: Annual Estimates of the Population by Age and Sex of White alone Not Hispanic" and "Table 4: Annual Estimates of the Population by Age and Sex of Hispanic or Latino Origin."

[52] Matthew D. Bramlett and William D. Mosher, "First Marriage Dissolution, Divorce, and Remarriage: United States," *Advance Data from Vital and Health Statistics*, no. 323 (Hyattsville, Maryland: National Center for Health Statistics, 2001), 1.

from family to family.

The dynamic for women changed quickly upon their arrival to Miami. The roles shifted and women have gained a new power identity that did not formerly exist for them, an independent identity that was not previously possible. According to many of the research participants, this is one of the factors that caused fear in their fathers and may have been one of the reasons why they sought out the attention of another woman, one he may control. The ability to control is a major factor for Hispanic G1 and G2 men in marriages. Loss of control over the wife threatens his position as the man.

This has impacted the view of marriage among the HH. Marriage is not taken lightly as many of the HH come from divorced homes. Many of them know the hurt and damage that divorce brought about and caused. When it comes to serious relationships, the HH can be as conservative as the G1s in that they desire a relationship that will last a lifetime. Most research participants sited the marriage of their grandparents, *abuelo* and *abuela*, as an example. This desire for real commitment was found among exiles, locals, and mobiles.

Raising the HH as Children

In a G1 home, the woman is the one primarily responsible for rearing children and maintaining the home. Since men are expected to generate income to support the home, he will be minimally involved in the rearing and development of the child. It may seem that the man does not love or does not care for wife and kids; this is not entirely true. This pattern stems back from their Latin American culture. G1 culture holds that a man is not good unless he can provide for his family. Therefore, his function is to provide as best as he can for his family. This, coupled with cost of living[53] in Miami and low pay scale, has led to G1 and G2 men often having more than one job. This consumption of time has created a gap in his ability to be involved in the life of the family. In G2 homes, women still have a great role in child rearing; however, these families tend to be double income households. Meaning, the financial responsibility is more equally distributed among the parents. As a result, both parents are able to be part of the home life. The research participants all shared about the challenges that their parents and grandparents underwent in the journey to arrive in the U.S.A. and then the process of starting over in Miami. Most HH stated that both parents had to work to provide sufficiently for their needs. This is one of the factors that has led to the emergence of the new family. Close-knit familial type relationships, "Framily," were formed in the absence of the traditional family.

Discipline in the typical HH home is expressed in two ways. First, it is

---

[53] Lisa Goetz, "Top Ten Most Expensive Cities in the U.S." June 13, 2017, accessed March 28, 2019, https://www.investopedia.com/articles/personal-finance/080916/top-10-most-expensive-cities-us.asp.

experienced through physical discipline. All of the research participants stated that their mother was the primary disciplinarian. If the father had to be in the physical discipline, it did not end well for that HH. For HH parents who are raising their children today, their forms of physical discipline are less drastic and more reflective of U.S.A. discipline forms. The second expression of discipline is humiliation. The research participants shared different forms of verbal and physical humiliation. This was often done in the presence of family or others for fullest affect. Some participants recalled specific moments when they were humiliated. HH homes do not normally include public humiliation as part of the disciplinary process. HH homes are more inclined to using practices such as "time out," or taking things away from the child.

Rites of Passage in the Family

For the Hispanic culture of Miami, the *"Quinces"* celebration is a pinnacle moment for the young lady. It is considered a coming of age moment for girls age 15. The Quinces celebration is the equivalent to the formal coming out into society as a young lady. The Quinces was used as the platform by which young ladies are presented as "ready" to the community. However, since its introduction and practice in Miami, the Quinces is seen mainly as a historic and cultural tradition. Many of the different Hispanic cultures in Miami have adopted this practice for their daughters. The Quinces moment is a syncretism of heritages today.

The researcher observed that the HH in Miami have demonstrated a willingness to adopt the best rites and traditions of the dominant cultures. The Quinces rite is an example that crosses all cultural lines. The only difference among the HH in their expression of the *Quince* rite is the level extravagance.

Figure 18. *Quinceañera* Presentation

Figure 19. ***Quinceañera*** **Father-Daughter Dance**

For mobiles, the *Quinces* may be quite the event, mirroring expenses of a wedding in some cases. Most banquet halls in Miami now include *Quince* celebration packages which include the dress, photography, entertainment, and all other amenities that would be associated with a wedding. The HH that seeks to hold to an ethnic identity is likely to host this kind of special event in their host country of origin so that the entire family can partake in it. For HH males, there is no formal passing of rites. Sexual activity is the one link that is closely associated towards manhood. This is generally true for mobiles, exiles, and all generations.

Death in the Family

The effect of death has a significant impact on the Hispanic home in Miami. The G1 may find the impact of death most difficult, especially when it happens to a family member in their home country. It is not uncommon for a G1 to not be present at the funeral or during the death process because of distance and location. A sense of separation and anxiety is common as the G1 is left to handle death alone or is left out of the family grieving process while death is occurring. Between G2s and HHs, the effect of death is felt mainly with the passing of the nuclear family or the passing of their new family. For the HH, death of family abroad is understood conceptually, yet with minimal remorse because there is no or minimal relationship established with that part of their family.

Hispanic Hybrids: Cultural Identity

Value Systems

The concept of *"Bien Educado"* and *"Mal Educado"* is crucial to understanding family dynamics in a HH home. Literally translated, these statements mean that one is either well educated or poorly educated. The dynamic equivalents of these terms are weightier than mere education. In Spanish *"bien educado"* refers to being brought up well, that is, that an individual's parents brought the individual up to be a well behaved, respectful person. This is a great sign of respect as it is a compliment that is paid not only to the child, but to the parents who reared that child. Conversely, to say that a child is *"mal educado"* is saying that the family did not fulfill its responsibility in terms of teaching an individual to behave properly. The HH understand that their behavior is a direct reflection on the entire family. One of the shared social and cultural characteristics among the research participants is that of family values and family care.

Strong family foundations are essential because they set the tone for how HH homes are and will continue to be formed in Miami. The research participants described the primary factors in determining what the Miami culture would deem *"bien"* or *"mal educado"* as matters of instilled family values, caring for children, education, and strong work ethic.

The research participants stated that political and economic hardships were essential to their family's journey and the unity it created for their home. This struggle has impacted behavior, values, and beliefs. Because the HH have not grown up in environments of political or economic turmoil, they recognize that part of the defining factors of unity and solidarity are expressed differently. This is one of the areas where the HH resembles the national cultural norm and have shared experience with nationals in regards to life satisfaction as most have never experienced a life other than that of the host culture. A perceived negative for children of HH is that because of their access to the privileges and opportunities in the U.S.A., their children are being affected negatively. They do not understand the challenges and work that has gone into the family being reestablished in Miami.

In the areas of life satisfaction and education, HH participants related primarily to the neighborhood of their ethnic composition. The HH expression in Miami is scattered across the forty-mile square. As each community varies, so does the HH composition that is found in each one.[54]

---

[54] John Berry, Jean Phinney, David Sam, and Paul Veddor, "Immigrant Youth: Acculturation, Identity, and Adaptation," *Applied Psychology: An International Review* 55, no. 3 (2006): 303-32.

Employment and Education

The HH in Miami is made up of different subsets of people coming from within the same country. Since approximately 67% of Miami Dade County is of Hispanic origin,[55] the subsets greatly vary in how a particular segment supports itself. There are a variety of factors that influence how or what one does for support. The greatest factor in determining how an HH supports the self is their legal status or lack thereof. This impacts ability to work, ability for housing, and access to government assistance. Research participants each articulated different expressions of challenges based on their parents and grandparent's ability to gain legal standing and employment.

G1s and G2s with previous education tended to excel further and faster than those without it. Education was a major factor for that original generation of immigrants as it determined potential for employment, culture and language learning. Current data demonstrates that of the 25 million Hispanics in the U.S.A., less than five million have a college education or more.[56] This often explains the reason behind why many Hispanics settle for lower paying jobs. The bilingual HH in Miami are considered high value potential employees outside of Miami. While most in Miami are bilingual, the majority of the U.S.A. population is not. If an HH ventures out of Miami, their ability to learn and earn more increases. For the HH who stays in Miami, there are many places, where pending the level of education and skill, one can find employment. Due to the fact that more residents in Miami speak Spanish more than any other language,[57] finding and keeping middle and upper level employment is a challenge. The market is saturated with educated bilingual persons, primarily G2s and the HH. Low income positions, while they are available, are also challenging to find and keep because of competition. The undocumented population of Miami is willing to do the same work for less income. Because of the cost of living, it is common to see multiple generations of family living in one home. Of those who qualified as research participants, six of the nine HHs are either currently living with their parents or were living with their parents within the last two years. These HHs are double income married households.

While the undocumented may have more difficulty in finding employment than those who are able to work legally, Miami has proven to be a favorable place to reside if one is undocumented. It is fairly common for undocumented persons to work within small restaurants, as fruit and water vendors, as knife sharpeners, home cleaners, or even as live in nannies. It is common for an

---

55 Miami-Dade County Profiles, American Community Survey, Department of Regulatory and Economic Resources | Planning Research and Economic Analysis Section, September 2017.

56 Patricia P. Martin, "Hispanics, Social Security, and Supplemental Security Income." Social Security Administration Office of Policy, 2007, accessed March 28, 2019, http://www.ssa.gov/policy/docs/ssb/v67n2/v67n2p73.html.

57 U.S.A. Census Bureau 2009.

immigrant to take a trade that he knew from his home country and apply it to Miami as best possible. HHs are not faced with the challenge of illegal employment because of their birth in the U.S.A.

Upon observation, HH of exiles are not likely to fully understand their parents' and grandparents' cultural identities or even the conditions of life that they left behind. For the HH, this is probably the clearest break in terms of "their" and "our" worldview. At the time of this writing, the subject of immigration is a high priority in the U.S.A. Thousands are marching towards the southern border in the form of caravans. Some are seeking a better life, others have questionable goals. The HH is conflicted in these matters. It is also conflicted with politics of their parents and grandparents. Some HH have become critical of new immigrants. Some HH are at odds politically with each other, despite their shared inter-ethnic backgrounds. While blood may be thicker than water, HH culture seems to be thicker than blood.

Social Structures

Since over 67% of Miami Dade's population is Hispanic, it can feel as if one is living abroad. Most of the research participants noted that one unique point to living in Miami is that it "has the feel of a Major Latin American City with access to North American commodities." The Hispanic population, G1–HH of Miami, are found in almost every neighborhood of Miami, with the exception of communities where there is a higher than normal concentration of other minorities: African Americans, Jews, and Haitians.

There are areas in Miami where poverty among Hispanics exists. However, since the G2s and HH live in close proximity to each other, the lines blur between low income, middle, upper income communities from one block to the next. In a few circumstances, there are pockets of persons with high concentrations of one country; this is not the rule, rather the exception. Miami as a whole is home to over 40 different Latin American cultures. This is one of the primary factors for the emergence of the HH; everyone blends with each other. While Miami is heterogeneous, living there feels homogenous for the HH: "we are one big group."

Taboos Found among the HH

Because of the blending of many cultures, some taboos that are true to most Latin cultures also exist. Dating or marrying a Black person is not accepted by G1s and is not normally embraced by G2s and some HHs. Among the three generations, there is a minimal integration, romantically or even socially. In Miami, where communities are primarily African American or Haitian, there is less than a 20% population of Hispanics present,[58] in comparison with the standard 67% found everywhere else in the county.

---

[58] City of Miami Planning Department.

HH women are frowned upon if they move out of their home prior to marriage. For G2s and HHs, moving out of the home for the purpose of education is better received today than in the past. Often times, young women will choose to stay for their education rather than leave for other universities to maintain the sense of order in the home. If a G2 or HH moves out to live with a mate, this too is looked down upon.

Pregnancy out of wedlock is also very embarrassing for the HH woman and her family. This is a point of shame for her and the home. Responses towards the HH vary from family expulsion for a season or in some extreme cases, the nuclear family will care for the daughter and may choose to cut all contact with the extended family to avoid further embarrassment. The new family then becomes the only family. Pregnancy out of wedlock is rising among Hispanics. It was noted that in 2013, 53% of all births to Hispanics in the U.S.A. were out of wedlock.[59] While sexual intimacy outside of wedlock is publicly condemned, it still happens and is continuing to occur. Worth noting, of the pregnancies outside of wedlock, the bulk of them occurred among the exile population of Hispanics. This indicates that HH exiles are falling into the historic disparity cycle that accompanies other minorities in the U.S.A.

Fetal terminations or abortions are viable options among HH mobiles. This group tends to be more economically secure, allowing them to access these kinds of services more readily. While this procedure is considered a major taboo in the Hispanic culture, it is a less shameful option to consider, as long as the rest of the family does not find out about it.

The issue of faith is one that can lead to turmoil among family that is present in Miami. Catholic roots run deep to most HH homes, especially among early generations. Leaving one's faith is viewed not only as a rejection of God, but also a rejection of one's family and culture. Common responses by family may include shunning or being ridiculed for joining a sect or abandonment of faith. The HH is open to matters of spirituality as a whole; they are quite tolerant groups as they are progressive in their North American ways and have been exposed to such a variety of faith by those living in and passing through Miami.

Perhaps the most tragic taboo is that of a child that declares themselves to be homosexual. It is particularly more shameful when it is a boy. Since the culture is *"machista"* in nature, a male who fails to marry, attempt to have children, and to carry on the family name, is considered a social and relational failure. If there is a son who openly chooses a homosexual relationship, he brings confusion and shame to the family. Consequences may include shunning, disowning, and complete separation from the nuclear and extended family. It is normal for the homosexual HH to develop his new family among

---

[59] Roger Clegg, "Latest Statistics on Out-of-Wedlock Births," *National Review,* October 11, 2013. https://www.nationalreview.com/corner/360990/latest-statistics-out-wedlock-births-roger-clegg.

other HH who are accepting of his sexual orientation.

Summary

In this chapter, the relational identities (i.e. marriage, family, child rearing practices) and cultural identity (i.e. value systems, employment and education, social structures, taboos) of Hispanic Hybrids are presented with ethnographic description. In the next chapter, missiological implications are derived from the research findings of this chapter.

Chapter 6

Missiological Implications of the Hispanic Hybrid Identity found in Miami-Dade County

Introduction

In this book, "Missiological implication" means "indirective derivation from research findings to have missiological significance" as illustrated by the classic work of Paul Hiebert.[60] By utilizing the Hofstede model, an American leadership practitioner can learn valuable information about leading in a foreign environment. The model allows practitioners to study nations like the ones in this research more in depth and make sound leadership judgments and recommendations culturally appropriate for that region. With the development of a HH Cultural Dimension, both professionals from the U.S.A. and Latin America coming into Miami may have a better understanding of the blends and differences that exist.

Implication of Ethnic Leadership in Miami and Beyond

The findings of this study on Hispanic Hybrid identity, will allow American and Latin American leaders to notice similarities and differences in preferred leadership styles between American and foreign populations.

Along with providing important insight about the Miami HH culture for leaders, the Cultural Dimensions model and ethnography in this case are also useful in providing helpful information to formulate recommendations for effective leadership practice by Americans and Latin Americans coming to Miami. Unfortunately, the history of leadership interactions between these nations has been poor, with the United States usually ignoring any need for cross-cultural awareness. Further research on cultural leadership practices with regards to this model could include an examination of the existing Americanized leadership theories and styles in an effort to strategically change or reshape their application to better serve in the context of a given culture, with special consideration for the cultural differences exposed and categorized by the Hofstede model.

While maintaining their own cultural values, Americans and Latin Americans operating in Miami should also recognize that cultural sensitivity and understanding through the implementation of leadership styles congruent with Miami's HH cultural dimensions is necessary to facilitate an effective

60 Paul G. Hiebert, The Missiological Implications of Epistemological Shifts: Affirming Truth in a Modern/post-modern World (Harrisburg, PA: Trinity Press International, 1999).

leadership process within its society.

Another possible missiological recommendation concerns the continued exploitation of Miami's natural resources to satisfy individualistic gains. To create an effective, beneficial international relationship between these nations, these countries must put aside personal market-centered desires and invest in helping each other to replenish their economies. As a long-term plan, this will pay off exponentially in partnership as the now depleted Latin American and flailing U.S.A. economies begin to flourish.

In addition, international assistance by U.S.A. based non-profit organizations, while beneficial in many instances for Latin America and Miami, must be presented in a way that is more culturally adaptive and less culturally invasive. The nationalistic cultural identity of the countries in this study is highly valued, and this must be protected. Applying culturally receptive leadership like this rather than trying to force Western leadership styles upon this diverse culture may be exactly the answer to issues in Latin America and some of the challenges found in Miami.

For those seeking to practice service, social, or faith-based work among the HH, one must and should consider a trans-ethnic leadership approach. In the following section, three critical components to leading and working among the HH will be highlighted. These principles are transferable to discipleship, church planting, outreach, and evangelism.

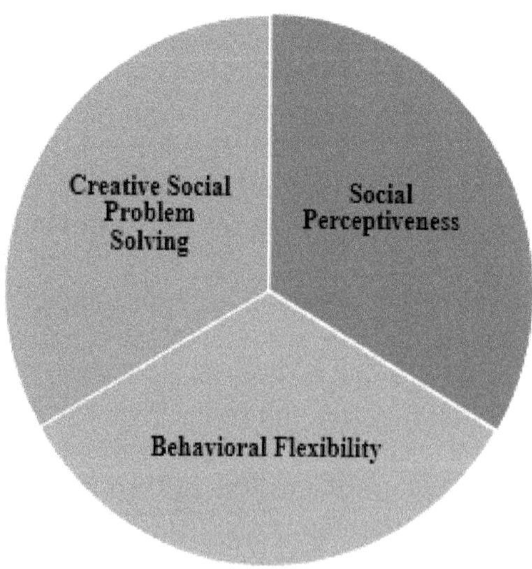

Figure 20. Essentials for Working Among and with the Hispanic Hybrid

Implication of Creative Social Problem-Solving

It has been stated that leadership is influence. Leaders must not only exercise influence, they must decide when, where, and how influence will be exercised to bring about the attainment of social goals. In trans-ethnic leadership, one must be able to demonstrate an ability to solve complex social problems in group dynamics. Trans-ethnic leadership problem solving differs from more routine problem solving in that the complexity, conflict, and change characterized in multicultural groups corroborates that leaders are presented with cultural challenges that are poorly defined. Ill-defined problems lack a single solution path: there may not be a right or wrong answer. These kinds of cultural challenges allow for the problem to be considered in a number of different ways. Defining the challenge to begin with may in actuality be the largest problem to clarify in order to work towards a resolution.

Complexity, novelty, and information ambiguity define one set of attributes that set apart leaders' problem-solving efforts. A trans-ethnic leader solves problems in "real-world" settings where time is short, and demands are many. As a result, these leaders will not have the luxury of analytically working through all options attached to a problem. Instead, they will have to generate solutions to multiple, rapidly unfolding problems, using short-cuts and applying general models. It will be common for most solutions to be extemporaneous, involving interactions among multiple problems as they unfold in a dynamic system.

Trans-ethnic leaders will need to be as fluid as the people who are coming and going across cultures, generations, and socio-economics. The leader must be able to adjust to each "season" in order to be effective across all the sub-cultural lines. One must have a disposition towards innovation. When the "season" changes, the leader must be able to develop and guide adaptive responses to new or changing situations. This leads to the notion that having a workable solution at the right time is far more important than having one truly best solution.61 This is true because of the seasonal challenges that impose time frames, conflicting goals, system demands, and limited resources.

This is most easily observed among the varying generations and political expression of the HH, specifically the Cuban HH. Many social values that cross generations are presently very fluid as there are conflicting opinions on working with the current Cuban government or seeking to re-establish an embargo between the U.S.A. and Cuba.[62] While the Cuban population of Miami is still opposed to the oppression that their people are enduring, the means by which they seek to protest that oppression is changing. The evidence is in the

---

[61] Edwin A. Fleishman, Francis Harding, Michael D. Mumford, and Stephen J. Zaccaro, "Leadership Skills for a Changing World: Solving Complex Social Problems," Leadership Quarterly 11, no. 1 (Spring 2000): 11-25.

[62] Ray Sanchez, "Miami's Cuban Exiles: The Widening Chasm between the Leadership and Newer Arrival," *Huffington Post* (Miami, FL), December 6, 2011.

desire to travel back to Cuba for the express purpose of visiting family at the expense of paying huge tariffs to the government. There has been a shift in the values among younger Cuban immigrants, G2s, and HHs. While politics matter, it is not the only thing that matters. Family, culture, music, and future seem to be the banner that this new generation is waving, even if it means doing business with the government against which the original generation protested. The trans-ethnic problem-solving leader will need to be able to grasp these kinds of cultural dynamics as they seek to lead among the HH.

Plans and executing strategy are critical. However, because the leader is working in a social context, social cognition and social implementation must take place for any leader to execute the strategy. If there is no collective "buy in" from the people, nothing will be accomplished. Thus, the leader must know the people and know how to persuade the people towards social response in fixing the problem. There must be a sense of "social negotiation" that occurs for communal response to take place. This requires flexibility in dealing with others and in adjusting plans opportunistically, as dictated by the demands of a changing social environment.

Social judgment skills are a key component to being able to aptly recognize and solve critical problems that are drenched in culture and subcultures. Being able to understand and observe social dynamics within the problem area represents a key leadership skill. Leaders must not only be able to formulate a plan that works within the context of the organization, they must also be able to implement this plan within a distinctly social context, marshaling support, communicating a vision, guiding team members, and motivating others.

An area where the trans-ethnic leader will be constantly seeking out solutions is that of immigration. Whether fair or not, all immigrants do not hold the same equal political standing although they may emigrate from the same general area of the world. The comparison between the Cuban and Haitian immigration is one example of this. Many Haitian American organizations have petitioned the U.S. Department of Human Services to speed up the visa approval process for family members, most of whom have been waiting for up to 12 years for a response.[63] Most of those waiting have either passed away or have become sick due to illnesses in Haiti such as cholera. The same is true for those seeking asylum in Cuba and other neighboring communities found in political, social, and economic unrest. The idea is to assist those in need and to better protect the closed borders of the U.SA.

---

[63] Steve Forester, "Haitian Diaspora Leaders Urge Haitian Family Reunification Program," Institute for Justice and Democracy in Haiti, August 18, 2014, http://www.ijdh.org/2014/08/topics/immigration-topics/73-haitian-american-diaspora-groups-and-leaders-urge-president-obama-to-create-a-haitian-family-reunification-parole-program/.

Implication of Social Perceptiveness

Self-Awareness

Key to trans-ethnic leadership is self-awareness: those who know who they are, what they stand for, and act with authenticity. The development of a well-formed identity will allow one to act courageously in any kind of setting where leadership is required. A high level of self-awareness will allow one to challenge the status quo and tactfully question the direction of others at similar and higher levels by standing up for what they believe. Self-awareness in relationship to others leads to authentic and genuine engagement. When one understands the other person, there is an appreciation of differing views that is established. This allows for both parties to be open to exploring new ways of seeing and experiencing the world. For those engaging in ministry among HH believers or the unchurched in Miami, this is essential.

The Greater Good

The trans-ethnic leader considers organizational decisions with a view to joint short-term gain as well as long-term impact in cooperation for the organization and society, keeping a clear view toward concurrent fiscal responsibility to the shareholders and a social responsibility to local communities and society.[64] There is no quick fix and overnight success for communal change, church planting, church growth, or impact. One must approach this as a marathon, not a sprint. The greater good of Miami has been and will be seen as a viable ministry option to consider.

Me-Focused vs. We-Centric Focus

Miami has developed a collective identity: a city built by immigrants, for immigrants. The trans-ethnic leader will foster a collective identity as necessary for the attainment of business results in the international setting. Building relational connections among all involved will develop a shared commitment to the mutually defined goals based on the greater good. The trans-ethnic leader will draw on the knowledge of collectivist cultures and build a "we-centric" focus uniquely suited for collaboration. Group success transcends autonomous actions. A challenge that one must be aware of is the existence of the hierarchical influence of Latin America and the recognition of individual performance that is promoted by North American culture.

---

[64] Beth Fisher-Yoshida, and Kathy D. Geller, Arête Leadership International Limited and FYI Fisher Yoshida International LLC, Lecture Series, 2007.

Voice and Dialogue

Dialogue offers an alternative approach to leader led discussions that by their implicit, hierarchical nature limit open interaction. Dialogue is a process that fosters inclusion, builds relationship, and gives a voice to a range of perspectives shared within a community orienting the group to consider. This allows for all perspectives to be acknowledged and considered. The process of dialogue honors difference through its emphasis on empathy, being able to see the world as the other does, by offering contextual and cultural insights to specific perspectives. This process creates a horizontal relationship out of which mutual trust is acquired. Once trust is acquired, movement towards a common goal will occur which will impact behavior, language, and values.

Language is at the heart of the HH in Miami. A trans-ethnic leader must be able to grasp and understand the use of both English and Spanish and the interplay that exists between those who are bicultural and bilingual. Both English and Spanish have influenced each other among the bilingual HH. There is a difference between Standard American English (SAE) and the English spoken in Miami. The English language has been influenced and incorporated among first and second-generation Cubans along with other minorities present. Improper English is quite often spoken in Miami; the same is true of the Spanish spoken as it has been influenced by the local culture.[65] Part of the result is the development of Spanglish.

Segregation Tensions

Segregation exists among the Hispanic Diaspora in Miami. This is felt socio-economically, educationally, racially, and through gender roles. There are many hierarchical challenges that exist among the Diaspora Hispanic peoples represented. Because of their backgrounds, education, and cultural association, some Hispanic communities seem to behave different towards others; many would contend that they are better or higher than others. This is the World Systems Theory[66] playing itself out.

First, in Miami, Southern-based racial-ethnic groups in the U.S.A. that are of honorary white status tend to possess greater human, social, and economic capital, which means they may have a greater means of assisting their homeland. Second, approaching the immigrant community from Southern nations that are in the semi periphery, they are in a better position to assist members of their ethnic kin in the U.S.A., either through capital and connections or simply through "status capital."[67] With this in mind,

---

[65] Kristen Mullen, "A Cross-Generational Analysis of Spanish to English Lexico-Semantic Phenomena in Emerging Miami English" (master's thesis, Florida International University, 2015).

[66] Christopher Chase-Dunn and Peter Grimes, "World-Systems Analysis," *Annual Review of Sociology* 21 (1995): 307-417.

[67] Rubin Patterson, "Social Forces," *Oxford Academic* 84, no. 4 (June 2006): 1891-1907.

development through strategic trans-ethnic leadership is bidirectional.

Behavioral Flexibility

Flexibility must be the operative word in this section. Working among any culture is a challenge. Working among converging cultures simultaneously is not any easier. In the following section, successful behaviors will be mentioned and expounded on that have demonstrated success by trans-ethnic leaders.[68]

Time orientation is an area that must be managed and tempered among the HH. Culturally, the HH in Miami are very time aware, though not time present. The distinction is this: "We will get to it when we get to it, but we know we need to get to it, so we will get to it...eventually." Timeliness is often one of those areas that pose challenges to those who come from "on-time" cultures. Thus, behavioral flexibility will be necessary in the areas of timeliness.

Uncertainty of the future is a state in which many exist. In part this is due to political instability, for some it is because of financial reasons, for others it is because of political turmoil, and lastly, many in Miami are not from Miami, therefore this is not truly home for a large percentage of the population. The idea of "long term" planning is redefined to a two to three-year window due to the transient nature of those who live there. These kinds of challenges will often build resiliency for the trans-ethnic leader. Resiliency will be necessary for the trans-ethnic leader in order to build on the differences and complexities of those living in Miami as this will allow them to function in equivocal environments.

Team conductivity and flexibility will be necessary for the trans-ethnic leader to succeed in Miami. With so many ethnicities present, cultural understanding of backgrounds will be key in team building and team work. By understanding where team members are coming from, leaders will be able not simply to understand them ethnically, but they will be able to work with their separate cultures towards a shared goal. This kind of conductivity will allow for work to occur across boundaries and borders by integrating and connecting activities and ideas from where they are conceived. This is not merely cultural flexibility, rather pragmatic flexibility. The trans-ethnic leader will seek to accept and integrate other cultures, both from within an organization and other cultures, to be able to adjust their values to other values and norms. Because cultural differences are taken into consideration, one leading in Miami must have an aptitude towards different cultures. This kind of perceptive responsiveness operates with a high degree of sensitivity to others' needs and values enabling the ability of the individual to function through intuition as much as fact.

---

68 Christine Springer, "Transnational Leadership Counts," *PA Times* 38 (September 2014), American Society for Public Administration, https://patimes.org/transnational-leadership-counts/.

Experience in a global setting clearly puts anyone working in a multiethnic environment ahead of the curve. An immersion experience living abroad, specifically somewhere in Latin America, will provide the trans-ethnic leader with a unique insight into a part of the fragmented community that is the Miami Diaspora. Living abroad has a major impact and influence on the way that one thinks and believes. A natural outcome will be that behaviors are defined and refined as one recognizes the power that is created through experience and immersion in different societies, cultures, and geographies. It is by an immersion experience that one recognizes the difference between diversity and inclusion. Diversity is the mix of people and things. Inclusion is making that mix work.[69]

It will be difficult for any one person to behave with excellence in the areas mentioned above. However, the stated qualities and characteristics are necessary and critical to trans-ethnic leadership. While no one will do all of the above well, what all can understand is the role of culture in translating the behaviors of leaders into effectiveness.

Areas Where Leadership is Under Represented and Deeply Needed

Social Fragmentation

Miami is a deeply fragmented community with distinct divides between the rich and poor and the many different cultures and ethnicities. With no overall vision or unifying leadership, feelings of isolation and suspicion abound. For the trans-ethnic leader in an organization, business, church, or non-profit, social fragmentation is inescapable. The question that the trans-ethnic leader must wrestle with is: How can Miami bridge the fragmented communities for a common goal? Most other cities that are heavily Hispanic populated are filled with primarily immigrants of Mexican descent. The future of the U.S.A. will include Mexican immigrants, and it will welcome immigrants from the rest of Latin America. The future of the U.S.A. will look like Miami in the coming decades.

Good Governance vs. Corruption

Miamians have long been disillusioned, and even embittered, with local government, as charges of corruption and wrong-doing surface repeatedly. Unfortunately, many patterns of Latin American government flowed into Miami as it becomes less about the welfare of the people and more about the benefit of the individual. While this is likely to be true across all political spheres, it is especially true in Miami among the Hispanic political leadership. The uncertain political climate makes business leaders wary of entering the public arena and becoming involved in debates of public issues. For trans-

[69] Springer.

ethnic leaders seeking to work in or with the political realm, they must be aware of the instability and lack of trust in politicians. This is a challenging arena as differing Hispanic peoples have varying degrees of status in the U.S.A.; it is not a Black and White issue nor is it an equal issue. While most politically involved may have started with the proper intent of working for and with Hispanics in Miami, most tend to go wayward for personal gain.[70]

Civic Engagement

In part stemming from a lack of good governance, many members of the community are indifferent about community-wide initiatives such as philanthropy, volunteering, and even voting. On average, only about 15 percent of eligible voters participate in Miami's municipal elections. This may be in part because most residents in Miami are not from there. Thus, there is a lack of interest or care in the betterment of the whole. Most Hispanics in Miami are there because it was a better option than staying in their home countries. However, if it were not for the instability of their homelands, they would have remained; most are openly vocal about that. There is little care for the city and its improvement. The Hispanic Diaspora is there for personal gain, not societal betterment. The trans-ethnic leader will need to understand the reasoning behind the arrivals of immigrants and challenge their thinking behind the concept of developing a new home. While Miami is not their old homeland, it is their new homeland; it will be the land of their children and grandchildren. Neglecting societal good will have generational implications.

Talent Retention

Miami needs bright young people to invest their talents in the community and view Miami as their long-term home. Trans-ethnic leaders will need to find ways to incubate and retain post-collegiate talent. If not, long term planning and societal betterment will remain in constant flux. This is where the leader must begin to think not simply about what he/she is doing today, but how to develop the next generation of leaders. The trans-ethnic leader will need to address the issue of retaining their superior young talent and provide incentives for them to invest in their community.

Education

Education is the foundation for building a globally competitive city. While graduation rates have improved, many local jobs are going unfilled and the unemployment rate remains high. Trans-ethnic leaders will need to be involved in the ongoing conversation of education acquisition. While the

---

70 Tony LoPresti, and Manuel Pastor, "Bringing Globalization Home: Lessons from Miami in Projecting the Voices of the People of Color and Connecting Global Forces to Local Problems," *Colorlines Magazine,* June 22, 2004.

diversity in Miami certainly lends itself towards being valuable in the work place outside of Miami, locally, the diversity is normal. This creates challenges for job development, opportunities, and placement.

Integrating Emerging Leaders into Existing Networks

The absence of young leadership at many companies and organizations is a significant challenge in Miami. Innovation and longevity are critical for building successful institutions. Trans-ethnic leaders will need to join forces to think beyond themselves and into the future of the city. Because of expense and transience, retention of the best and brightest will be an ongoing challenge. A way to address this matter will be through future collaboration in the public and private sectors.

Local initiatives in infrastructure and economic development have the greatest impact when the public and private sectors collaborate. One of Miami's most pressing challenges is in building the cooperation between public institutions and private companies to create opportunities for growth and to counter fragmentation. Trans-ethnic leaders will need to address the political and socio-economic barriers that exist in order to develop cross-functional partnerships. This would allow for the individual leader to flourish, economic development to occur, and the city to benefit in every direction; everyone wins.

Summary

In chapters 4 and 5, ethnographic descriptions of the Hispanic Hybrid identity were presented by interpreting the collected data. In this chapter, missiological implications were derived from the ethnographic descriptions and here offered to be considered by practitioners.

Chapter 7

Recommendations for Those Thinking of Coming to Miami

To develop transnational leaders, organizations or individuals would do well to take on international assignments and cross-cultural exchange opportunities. The earlier that these experiences are offered in one's career, the longer lasting and more accelerated the development will be. Both short and long-term expatriate assignments, job swaps, internships, and long-duration travel assignments should be developed that allow employees to spend time in unfamiliar countries and cultures.

In order to accelerate current trans-ethnic leadership growth and capabilities, organizational exchanges and interventions should be elevated to deliberately change the nature of employee assignments to ensure that they are globally complex as well as involving cross-border assignments that present multicultural and diverse team challenges and experiential events that shape and cultivate cultural sensitivity. By doing so, the organization assists developing leadership with uncovering their values and taking ownership of talent development rather than simply relying on the human resource department.

To create a nurturing and sustaining multicultural global environment, leaders should be encouraged to take on new roles from which they personally will benefit and that will allow them to address risks through support and networking on the ground. Assignments in this area that generally turn out to be positive are those for which the organization provides assistance in making adjustments, either through assigned mentors, networking, or on-the-ground leadership connections.

Having and developing trans-ethnic leaders within is a critical component of success of any organization, business, non-profit, and especially church. Organizations must maintain a consistent focus on the issue of global talent, develop and communicate regularly on the progress and quality of talent, and make global assignments real career enhancers that talented employees aspire to participate in as a way to accelerate their careers.[71]

---

[71] Springer.

APPENDIX 1

CONSENT TO PARTICIPATE IN RESEARCH

I understand that I am being asked to participate in a research study conducted by J. David Lopez, a student from Western Seminary. The study is being conducted as part of his Doctor of Intercultural Studies Dissertation. I have been informed about the following concerning the research:

Purpose of the Study

To describe one's general understanding of family, education, values, work, and how the blending of cultures has impacted them.

Procedures

If you volunteer to participate in this study, you will be asked to take part in three interviews that will last approximately 45-60 minutes each.

Potential Risks and Discomforts

None.

Confidentiality

Any information that is obtained in connection with this study and that can be identified with you, will remain confidential and will be disclosed only with your permission or as required by law. Confidentiality will be maintained.

If the interview is to be digitally recorded, it will be protected by password. Only the researcher has the password to gain access to the digital copy.

Participation and Withdrawal

You can choose whether or not to be in this study. If you volunteer to be in this study, you may withdraw at any time without consequences of any kind or loss of benefits to which you are otherwise entitled. You may also refuse to answer any questions you do not want to answer. There is no penalty if you withdraw from the study and you will not lose any benefits to which you are otherwise entitled.

I understand the procedures described above. My questions have been answered to my satisfaction, and I agree to participate in this study. I have been given a copy of this form.

Interviewer: ______________________________ Date: _______________

Participant Signature: ______________________ Date: _______________

APPENDIX 2

SAMPLE SURVEY

The purpose of this survey is to assist J. David Lopez, a student from Western Seminary. You are being asked to participate in a brief study on Hispanics in Miami. This information is confidential and will not be for public use. Any information that is shared will be done anonymously. Survey design is by the ACS.[72]

What is your first and last name?
What is your marital status?

- Married
- Widowed
- Divorced
- Separated

Have you ever been divorced?

- Yes
- No

Where were you born?

- City
- Country

What is the highest degree or level of school you have ever completed?

- No schooling completed
- Nursery school
- Kindergarten
- Grade 1-11
- 12th grade no diploma
- Regular high school diploma
- GED or alternative credential
- Some college credit, but less than 1 year of college credit
- 1 or more years of college credit, no degree
- Associate's degree
- Bachelor's degree
- Master's degree
- Professional degree beyond a bachelor's degree
- Doctorate degree

---

[72] United States Census Bureau, "American Community Survey," 2010.

What is your race?

- White
- Black, African American, or Negro
- American India or Alaskan Native
- Some other race, please print ___________

How long have you lived in Miami? _____(Years)
Do you have any children? If so, how many? Yes No
Which country does your family originate from? If multiple, which are they? (Example: My father is from Spain, my mother is from Costa Rica.)
Are you legally able to work?

- Yes
- No

Are you currently employed?

- Yes
- No

Your combined household income is between:

- $0-$25,000
- $25,000 - $45,000
- $45,000 - $65,000
- $65,000 - $85,000
- $85,000 - $100,000
- $100,000 +

Are you of Hispanic, Latino, or Spanish Origin?

- No, not of Hispanic, Latino, or Spanish Origin
- Yes, Mexican, Mexican American, Chicano
- Yes, Puerto Rican
- Yes, Cuban
- Yes, another Hispanic Latino, or Spanish origin – for example, Argentinean, Colombian, Dominican, Nicaraguan, Salvadorian, Spaniard, and so on: ______________

I identify myself as Hispanic.

- Strongly disagree
- Disagree
- Neutral
- Agree
- Strongly agree

I identify myself as American.

- Strongly disagree
- Disagree
- Neutral

- Agree
- Strongly agree

Do you speak a language other than English at home?

- If yes, which is it? ____________
- No (you are done)

How well do you speak this other language?

- Very well
- Well
- Not well
- Not at all

APPENDIX 3

SAMPLE ETHNOGRAPHIC RESEARCH QUESTIONS

Descriptive Questions

- Could you tell me more about yourself? (single/married/employed/etc.)
- Could you tell me about your family background? Where are they from? How long have they been in the U.S.A?
- How do you describe yourself ethnically?
- Can you tell me what it means to be (your ethnicity)?
- Can you tell me what it means to be American?
- What were some defining moments for you in terms of cultural/ethnic definition (American or not)?
- Are you bilingual? If so, when do you choose to use one language over the other?
- How would describe the different kinds of Hispanics who are blending in Miami? What do you like? Dislike?
- What has it been like growing up as a/or around Hispanic Hybrids in Miami? Challenges? Benefits?
- How do you think it will be different for your children?
- If you have children, what difference have you seen in their ethnic upbringing when compared to yours?

Structural Questions

- If I would have grown up with you, what would I have experienced? What was it like growing up for you in Miami?
- What was it like being part of a family for you? (Are they all Hispanics as well?)
- What did structure look like for you? Who instituted structure?
- What was school like for you?
- At what point/age would you say you "grew up?" Why then? What happened?
- Which, if any of the questions mentioned above, would you say can be "shared" responses for other Hispanics in Miami? Why?

Contrast Questions:

- What's the distinction between you and other Hispanics from different ethnic backgrounds?
- What's the difference between you and other Americans?
- What do you believe is different in your own up brining?

- What do you believe will be different about the way your children are brought up? (behavior/values/instruction, etc.)

Bibliography

Associated Press. "Whites will no longer be a majority in U.S. by 2043 as Hispanic population surges, Census data reveals." *Daily Mail* (UK), December 12, 2012. https://www.dailymail.co.uk/news/article-2247119/2043-census-prediction-US-whites-longer-majority-Hispanic-population-surges.html.

Berry, John and Jean Phinney, David Sam, and Paul Vedder. "Immigrant Youth: Acculturation, Identity, and Adaptation." *Applied Psychology: An International Review* 55, no. 3 (2006): 303-32.

Bouvier, Leon F. and John L. Martin. "Shaping Florida: The Effects of Immigration." Center for Immigration Studies, Low Immigration and Pro-Immigration (1995). http://cis.org/FloridaImmigrants19702020.

Bramlett, Matthew D. and William D. Mosher. "First Marriage Dissolution, Divorce, and Remarraige: United States." *Advance Data from Vital and Health Statistics,* no. 323. Hyattsville, Maryland: National Center for Health Statistics (May 31, 2001).

Bronfenbrenner, Urie. "Ecological Systems Theory." In *Annals of Child Development.* Vol. 6. Edited by Ross Vasta. *International Encyclopedia of Education.* Edited by Torsten Husen and T. Neville Postlewaite. London: Jessica Kingsley Publisher, 1989.

Chase-Dunn, Christopher and Peter Grimes. "World-Systems Analysis." *Annual Review of Sociology* 21 (1995): 387-417.

Clegg, Roger. "Latest Statistics on Out-of-Wedlock Births." *National Review,* October 11, 2013. https://www.nationalreview.com/corner/360990/latest-statistics-out-wedlock-births-roger-clegg/.

Contini, Rina Manuela. "New Generations and Intercultural Integration in Multi-Ethnic Society." *Procedia – Social and Behavioral Sciences* 93 (October 2013): 1819-1829. https://doi.org/10.1016/j.sbspro.2013.10.124.

Costigan, C. L., C. M. Koryzma, J. M. Hua, and L. J. Chance. "Ethnic Identity, Achievement, and Psychological Adjustment: Examining Risk and Resilience among Youth from Immigrant Chinese Families in Canada." *Cultural Diversity and Ethnic Minority Psychology* 16, no. 2 (April 2010): 264–73. https://doi.org/10.1037/a0017275.

Creswell, John W. "Steps in Conducting a Scholarly Mixed Methods Study." Presentation November 14, 2013, DigitalCommons@University of Nebraska – Lincoln. Accessed April 1, 2020. https://digitalcommons.unl.edu/dberspeakers/48/.

Fisher-Yoshida, Beth and Kathy D. Geller. Arête Leadership International Limited and FYI Fisher Yoshida International LLC. Lecture Series, 2007.

Fleishman, Edwin A., Francis Harding, Miachael D. Mumford, Stephen J. Zaccaro. "Leadership Skills for a Changing World: Solving Complex Social Problems." *Leadership Quarterly* 11, no. 1 (Spring 2000): 11-25.

Florida Vital Statistics of Marriage and Divorce. 2009. http://www.vitalstats@flheath.gov/.

Forester, Steve. "Haitian Diaspora Leaders Urge Haitian Family Reunification Program." Institute for Justice and Democracy in Haiti, August 18, 2014. http://www.ijdh.org/2014/08/topics/immigration-topics/73-haitian-american-diaspora-groups-and-leaders-urge-president-obama-to-create-a-haitian-family-reunification-parole-program/.

Gates, David et al. "A Taste of Salsa."*Newsweek*, January 19, 1998. Academic Search Premier, EBSCO.

Gobin, Emma and Géraldine Morel. "Ethnography and Religious Anthropology of Cuba: Historical and Bibliographical Landmarks." *Ateliers d'anthropologie* 38 (2013). https://doi.org/10.4000/ateliers.9447.

Goetz, Lisa. "Top 10 Most Expensive Cities in the U.S." June 13, 2017. Accessed March 28, 2019. https://www.investopedia.com/articles/personal-finance/080916/top-10-most-expensive-cities-us.asp.

Guisepi, R. A. and Various Authors. "Hispanic Americans." *History World International.* Accessed March 28, 2019. http://history-world.org/hispanics.html.

Guttmacher Institute, Alan. "Abortion in Women's Lives." Washington D.C.: AGI, 2006.

Hall, E. T. *The Dance of Life, the Other Dimension of Time.* London: Anchor Books, 1989.

Haller, William and Patricia Landolt. "The Transnational Dimensions of Identity Formation: Adult Children of Immigrants in Miami." *Ethnic and Racial Studies* 28, no. 6 (November 2005): 1182-1214. https://doi.org/10.1080/01419870500224554.

Hedinger, Mark and Enoch Wan. "Understanding 'Relationality' from a Trinitarian Perspective." *Global Missiology, Trinitarian Studies* (January 2006). www.globalmissiology.org.

Hiebert, Paul G. *The Missiological Implications of Epistemological Shifts: Affirming Truth in a Modern/post-modern World.* Harrisburg, PA: Trinity Press International, 1999.

Hinze, Malena. "The Revolutionary Role of Women in Cuba." *Liberation,* March 1, 2006. https://www.liberationnews.org/06-03-01-the-revolutionary-role-women-in-html/.

Hofstead, G. and G. J. Hofstede. *Cultures and Organizations: Software of the Mind.* New York, NY: McGraw-Hill, 2004.

Hofstede Center, The. "National Culture." (n.d.): http://geert-hofstede.com/national-culture.html.

Hofstede Insights. *Costa Rica Cultural Dimension*. Accessed March 28, 2019 https://www.hofstede-insights.com/country/costa-rica/

_______. *Colombia Cultural Dimension*. Accessed March 28, 2019. https://www.hofstede-insights.com/country/colombia/.

_______. *The Six Dimensions of National Culture.* Accessed March 28, 2019. https://www.hofstede-insights.com/models/national-culture/.

_______. *United States Cultural Dimension*. Accessed March 28, 2019. https://www.hofstede-insights.com/country/the-usa/.

Kennedy, John F. Presidential Library and Museum. "The Bay of Pigs." Accessed March 28, 2019. https://www.jfklibrary.org/learn/about-jfk/jfk-in-history/the-bay-of-pigs.

Kraidy, Marwan M. *Hybridity or the Cultural Logic of Globalization.* Philadelphia, PA: Temple University Press, 2005.

Krogstad, Jens Manuel. "Key Facts about how the U.S. Hispanic Population is Changing." Pew Research Center, Washington D.C. (September 8, 2016). https://www.pewresearch.org/fact-tank/2016/09/08/key-facts-about-how-the-u-s-hispanic-population-is-changing/.

Krogstad, Jens Manuel, Renee Stepler and Mark Hugo Lopez. "English proficiency on the rise among latinos." Pew Research Center, Washington D.C. (May 12, 2015). http://www.pewhispanic.org/2015/05/12/english-proficiency-on-the-rise-among-latinos/.

Likert, Rensis. "Likert Scale: A psychometric scale commonly invovled in research that employs questionnaires by using fixed choice response formats and is designed to measure attitudes or opinions." 1997.

Lopez, J. David. "An Ethnographic Study of the Hispanic Hybrid Identity in Miami." PhD diss., Western Seminary, Portland, OR, 2019.

LoPresti, Tony and Manuel Pastor. "Bringing Globalization Home: Lessons from Miami in Projecting the Voices of the People of Color and Connecting Global Forces to Local Problems." *Colorlines Magazine* , June 22, 2004.

Marshall, S. "Ethnic Socialization of African American Children: Implications for Parenting, Identity Development, and Acadmic Achievement." *Journal of Youth and Adolescence,* 24, no. 4 (August 1995): 377-96.

Martin, Patricia P. "Hispanics, Social Security, and Supplemental Security Income." Social Security Administration Office of Policy. 2007. Accessed March 28, 2019. https://www.ssa.gov/policy/docs/ssb/v67n2/v67n2p73.html.

Mason, S. J. "L'Église ouverte sur le monde." *Nouvelle Revue Théologiquê,* (1962): 84.

Mazzei, Patricia. "South Florida ranks No. 5 in undocumented immigrant population, study finds." *Miami Herald,* February 2, 2017. https://www.miamiherald.com/news/politics-government/article131785114.html.

Miami-Dade County Profiles. American Community Survey. Department of Regulatory and Economic Resources | Planning Research and Economic Analysis Section. September 2017.

Moje, E. B. et al. "Working Toward Third Space in Content Area Literacy: An Examination of Everyday Funds of Knowldege and Discourse." *Reading Research Quarterly* 38 (2004): 38-70.

Montenegro, S. "Nicaragua's Sexual Culture: A Loveless Legacy." *Revista Envio* 240 (July 2001). http://www.envio.org.ni/articulo/1515.

Mullen, Kristen. "A Cross-Generational Analysis of Spanish to English Lexico-Semantic Phenomena in Emerging Miami English." Master's thesis, Florida International University, 2015.

Neumann, Caryn E. "Cuban Immigrants." *Immigration to the United States.* Accessed March 28, 2019. http://immigrationtounitedstates.org/453-cuban-immigrants.html.

Nijman, Jan. "Locals, Exiles, and Cosmopolitans: A Theoretical Argument about Identity and Places in Miami." *Journal of Economic and Social Geography* 98, no. 2 (April 2007): 176-87. https://doi.org/10.1111/j.1467-9663.2007.00390.x.

_______. *Miami: Mistress of the Americas.* Philadelphia: University of Pennsylvania Press, 2011.

Nogle, June M. and Stanley K. Smith. "An Evaluation of Hispanic Population Estimates." *Social Science Quarterly* (2004): 742.

Pane, Debra M. "Third Space Theory: Reconceptualizing Content Literacy Learning." *ResearchGate* (2005): 1-12.

Parke, R. D. and R. Buriel. "Socialization in the Family: Ecological and Ethnic Perspectives." In *Handbook of Child Psychology,* edited by W. Damon, vol. 3. New York, NY: Wiley Publishers, 1998.

Patterson, Rubin. "Social Forces." *Oxford Academic* 84, no. 4 (June 2006): 1891-1907.

Phinney, J. S. "Ethnic Identity and Acculturation." In *Acculturation: Advances in Theory, Measurement, and Applied Research,* edited by K. Chun, P. Organista, and G. Marin. Washington, DC: American Psychological Association, 2003.

Power, John. *History of Salvation: Introducing the Old Testament.* Dublin: MacMillan, 1967.

Ripley, C. Peter. *Conversations with Cuba.* Athens, GA: The University of Georgia Press, 1999.

Sabogal, F., G. Marın, R. Otero-Sabogal, B. Marın, and E. J. Perez-Stable. "Hispanic Familism and Acculturation: What Changes and What Doesn't?" *Hispanic Journal of Behavrioral Sciences* 9, no. 4 (December 1987): 397–412. https//doi.org/10.1177/07399863870094003.

Sanchez, Ray. "Miami's Cuban Exiles: The Widening Chasm Between the Leadership and Newer Arrivals." *Huffington Post* (Miami, FL), December 6, 2011.

Spradley, James P. *Participant Observation.* New York: Holt, Rhinehart & Winston Inc., 1980.

Springer, Christine. "Transnational Leadership Counts." *PA Times* 38 (September 2014), American Society for Public Administration. https://patimes.org/transnational-leadership-counts/.

Stavans, Ilan. *The American Prospect Quarterly Magazine*, Fall 1993.

Stepick, Alex and Alejandro Portes. *City On the Edge: The Transformation of Miami*. Los Angeles: University of California Press, 1993.

Thomson, Maria D. and Laurie Hoffman-Goetz. "Defining and measuring acculturation: A systematic review of public health studies with Hispanic populations in the United States." *Social Science & Medicine* 69, no. 7 (October 2009): 983-91. https://doi.org/10.1016/j.socscimed.2009.05.011.

Trimmer, Michael. "Why are US Hispanics defecting from Catholic to Evangelical churches?" *Christianity Today*, May 5, 2014. https://www.christiantoday.com/article/us-hispanics-are-leaving-catholic-churches-for-evangelical-ones/37287.htm.

UNICEF (2006). UNICEF Nicaragua. *United for Children*. Retrieved November 8, 2009. Accessed March 28, 2019. http://www.unicef.org/index.php.

United States Census Bureau. "American Community Survey." Census. 2010.

United States Census Bureau. "Facts for Features: Hispanic Heritage Month 2016." CB16-FF.16. October 12, 2016. http://www.census.gov/newsroom/facts-for-features/2016/cb16-ff16.html.

United States Census Bureau. "Facts for Features: Hispanic Heritage Month 2017." August 31, 2017. https://www.census.gov/newsroom/facts-for-features/2017/hispanic-heritage.html.

United States Department of Health and Human Services, Administration for Children and Families, Office of Refugee Resettlement. The Refugee Act of 1980, Public Law 96-212, March 17, 1980. Last reviewed May 15, 2019. Accessed March 28, 2019. https://www.acf.hhs.gov/orr/resource/the-refugee-act.

United States Department of Labor. "Hispanics and Latinos in industries and occupations." October 9, 2015. https://www.bls.gov/opub/ted/2015/hispanics-and-latinos-in-industries-and-occupations.htm.

University Center for International Studies [UCIS] (2004). "Family Life in Nicaragua: Illuminations: Cultural Formations of the Americas." Retrieved September 28, 2009. Accessed March 28, 2019. http://www.ucis.pitt.edu/clas/nicaragua_proj/society/Family/Soc-familylife.pdf.

Vertovec, Steven. "Migration and other Modes of Transnationalism: Toward Conceptual Cross-Fertilization." *International Migration Review* 37, no. 3 (Fall 2003): 641-65. https://doi.org/10.1111/j.1747-7379.2003.tb00153.x.

Waldinger, Roger D. "Between "Here" and "There": Immigrant Cross-border Activities and Loyalties." *International Migration Review* 42, no. 1 (March 2008): 3-29. https://doi.org/10.1111/j.1747-7379.2007.00112.x.

Weaver, Laurie and Judith Marquez. "Characteristics of Hispanic Families." Presentation, University of Houston – Clear Lake, n.d.

www.ingramcontent.com/pod-product-compliance
Ingram Content Group UK Ltd.
Pitfield, Milton Keynes, MK11 3LW, UK
UKHW020422250726
13987UKWH00007B/2774

9 781954 692046